Joy Church
P.O. Box 247
Mount Juliet, TN 37121
www.joychurch.net

Printed in the United States of America
Publisher's Cataloging-in-Publication data
Frease, Jim.
Wisdom 365: A daily dose of wisdom because the decisions you make today will directly affect your tomorrow. / Jim Frease
p. 384
ISBN 978-0-9983918-8-5
1. Motivational 2. Inspirational. 3. Christian Living.
First Edition
First Printing 2019

JIM FREASE

WISDOM 365

A DAILY DOSE OF WISDOM

*Because the decisions you make today
will directly affect your tomorrow.*

This book is dedicated
to the people of Joy Church.
I am honored to be your pastor.

I love and believe in you!

INTRODUCTION

This collection of wisdom nuggets revolves entirely around the Book of Proverbs. The word "proverb" in the Hebrew language means a rule or standard. It's not a rule or standard that will bring condemnation into your life if you don't live up to it. It's a rule or standard that will enhance your standard of living if you apply it to your life.

These proverbs will bring you wisdom. The Hebrew word for wisdom literally means "skilled living." Therefore, once you apply these proverbs to your life, it will enhance your relationships, marriage, parenting, purpose, finances, health, joy, peace, and decision-making.

The Bible says in Proverbs 4:7, *"Wisdom is the principal thing, therefore get wisdom."* This book is designed to take verses from Proverbs and match them with my wisdom nuggets in a way that illustrates the principle in the proverb.

You are the sum total of the decisions you make. Who you are today is a direct result of your choices yesterday. Therefore, the decisions you are making today directly affect your tomorrow!

This book is designed to enhance your decision making, raise your standard of living, and give you wisdom 365 days of the year.

JANUARY

I

The proverbs of Solomon
the son of David, king of Israel:
To know wisdom and instruction,
to perceive the words of understanding,
to receive the instruction of wisdom,
justice, judgment, and equity.
To give prudence to the simple, to the
young man knowledge and discretion.
Proverbs 1:1-4

THERE IS AN
OLDER VERSION OF YOU
COUNTING ON YOU TO
MAKE THE RIGHT CHOICES
TODAY

To give prudence to the simple,
to the young man
knowledge and discretion.

Proverbs 1:4

KNOWLEDGE BRINGS CONFIDENCE, AND CONFIDENCE IS THE BREEDING GROUND WHERE FAITH CAN FLOURISH.

A wise man will hear
and increase learning,
and a man of understanding
will attain wise counsel.

Proverbs 1:5

DON'T BE A KNOW-IT-ALL.

BE A LEARN-IT-ALL.

The fear of the LORD
is the beginning of knowledge,
but fools despise wisdom and instruction.

Proverbs 1:7

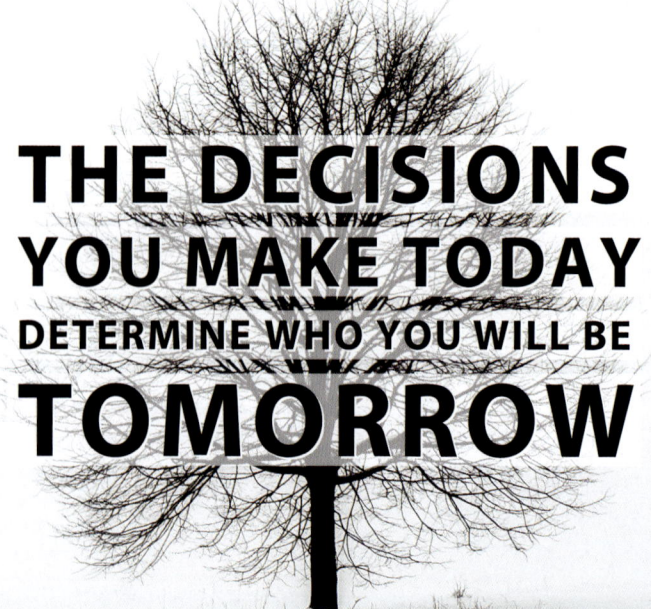

**THE DECISIONS
YOU MAKE TODAY
DETERMINE WHO YOU WILL BE
TOMORROW**

JANUARY

5

Turn at my rebuke.
Surely I will pour out my spirit on you.
I will make my words known to you.
Proverbs 1:23

IT'S NEVER TOO LATE TO BE
WHAT YOU MIGHT HAVE BEEN

For the turning away of the simple
will slay them, and the complacency of fools
will destroy them.

Proverbs 1:32

FACING DIFFICULTIES
IS INEVITABLE.
LEARNING FROM THEM
IS OPTIONAL.

But whoever listens to me
will dwell safely and will be secure,
without fear of evil.

Proverbs 1:33

FEAR
STOPS YOU FROM
TAKING ADVANTAG
OF A GOD-GIVEN
OPPORTUNITY

Discretion will preserve you.
Understanding will keep you.
Proverbs 2:11

DISCRETION

IS THE ABILITY TO
SEE THE HARVEST
BEFORE YOU
SOW THE SEED

For her house leads down to death,
and her paths to the dead.
None who go to her return,
nor do they regain the paths of life.
Proverbs 2:18-19

A "PATH" IS A ROAD
THAT WILL LEAD TO A
PREDICTABLE OUTCOME

YOU ARE NOT
THE EXCEPTION
TO THAT PATH

My son, do not forget my law,
but let your heart keep my commands.
For length of days and long life
and peace they will add to you.

Proverbs 3:1-2

THE INPUT OF
GOD'S WORD
will always produce
THE OUTCOME OF
A CHANGED LIFE

JANUARY

11

My son, do not forget my law,
but let your heart keep my commands.
For length of days and long life
and peace they will add to you.
Proverbs 3:1-2

GOD'S WORD IS NOT JUST INFORMATIONAL BUT TRANSFORMATIONAL

My son, do not forget my law,
but let your heart keep my commands.
For length of days and long life
and peace they will add to you.

Proverbs 3:1-2

If you give God
the first part
of your day,
you will
act on life
instead of
reacting to life.

Let not mercy and truth forsake you.
Bind them around your neck,
write them on the tablet of your heart,
and so find favor and high esteem
in the sight of God and man.

Proverbs 3:3-4

FAVOR IS NOT GOD
TALKING TO YOU

FAVOR IS GOD
TALKING TO
SOMEONE ELSE
ABOUT YOU

JANUARY

14

Let not mercy and truth forsake you.
Bind them around your neck,
write them on the tablet of your heart,
and so find favor and high esteem
in the sight of God and man.

Proverbs 3:3-4

YOU WILL
ALWAYS HAVE
A PERIOD
OF TIME OF
DOING
WHAT'S
RIGHT
BEFORE
SEEING
WHAT'S
RIGHT

Let not mercy and truth forsake you.
Bind them around your neck,
write them on the tablet of your heart,
and so find favor and high esteem
in the sight of God and man.

Proverbs 3:3-4

LEARN TO MAKE
THE RIGHT DECISIONS
IN THE WRONG CIRCUMSTANCES

JANUARY
16

Trust in the LORD with all your heart,
and lean not on your own understanding.
In all your ways acknowledge Him,
and He shall direct your paths.
Proverbs 3:5-6

THERE IS A BIG
DIFFERENCE BETWEEN

SURRENDERING
CONTROL

AND

RELINQUISHING
RESPONSIBILITY

Trust in the LORD with all your heart,
and lean not on your own understanding.
In all your ways acknowledge Him,
and He shall direct your paths.

Proverbs 3:5-6

DON'T LOOK AT WHAT YOU'RE
GOING THROUGH

LOOK AT WHAT YOU'RE
GOING TO

JANUARY

18

Trust in the LORD with all your heart,
and lean not on your own understanding.
In all your ways acknowledge Him,
and He shall direct your paths.
Proverbs 3:5-6

ONE OF THE GREATEST QUESTIONS
YOU CAN ASK GOD IS

"WHAT IS MY NEXT STEP?"

Honor the LORD with your possessions
and with the firstfruits of all your increase,
so your barns will be filled with plenty,
and your vats will overflow with new wine.

Proverbs 3:9-10

LIFE IS NOT ABOUT HOW MUCH YOU GET

BUT HOW MUCH YOU GIVE AWAY

JANUARY

20

My son, do not despise the chastening of the LORD, nor detest His correction. For whom the LORD loves He corrects, just as a father the son in whom he delights.

Proverbs 3:11-12

WHEN WE MAKE POOR CHOICES, WE TEND TO RUN TO PERMISSION, NOT CORRECTION

Happy is the man who finds wisdom and the man who gains understanding.

Proverbs 3:13

IT'S NOT HAPPY PEOPLE
WHO ARE THANKFUL

IT'S THANKFUL PEOPLE
WHO ARE HAPPY

Happy is the man who finds wisdom
and the man who gains understanding.
Proverbs 3:13

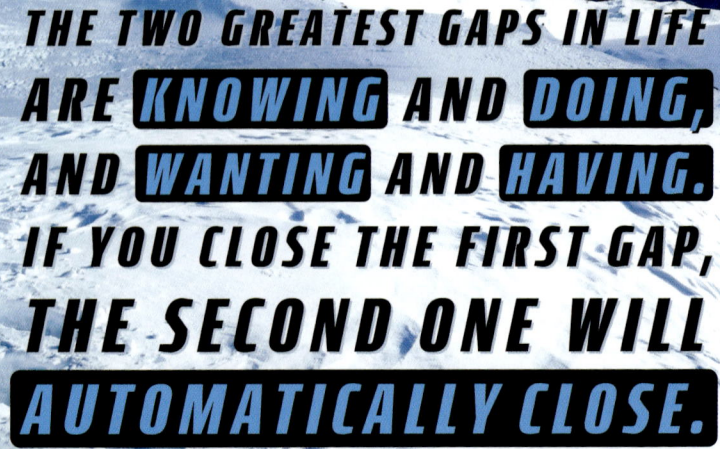

THE TWO GREATEST GAPS IN LIFE ARE KNOWING AND DOING, AND WANTING AND HAVING. IF YOU CLOSE THE FIRST GAP, THE SECOND ONE WILL AUTOMATICALLY CLOSE.

Happy is the man who finds wisdom
and the man who gains understanding,
for her proceeds are better than the profits
of silver and her gain than fine gold.
She is more precious than rubies, and all the
things you may desire cannot compare with her.
Length of days is in her right hand,
in her left hand riches and honor.

Proverbs 3:13-16

God wants to raise your standard of living so He can raise your standard of giving.

Her ways are ways of pleasantness,
and all her paths are peace.
She is a tree of life
to those who take hold of her,
and happy are all who retain her.

Proverbs 3:17-18

You will be demoted by

the problems you create

and promoted by

the problems

you solve

My son, let them not depart from your eyes.
Keep sound wisdom and discretion.

Proverbs 3:21

ANYTHING GAINED MUST BE MAINTAINED

So they will be life to your soul
and grace to your neck.

Proverbs 3:22

GRACE IS NOT
THE POWER OF GOD
TO OVERLOOK SIN.
GRACE IS THE POWER OF GOD
TO OVERCOME SIN.

When you lie down, you will not be afraid;
Yes, you will lie down
and your sleep will be sweet.

Proverbs 3:24

FEAR OPENS THE DOOR TO THE DEVIL
AND SHUTS THE DOOR TO GOD.

FAITH OPENS THE DOOR TO GOD
AND SHUTS THE DOOR TO THE DEVIL.

Do not be afraid of sudden terror,
nor of trouble from the wicked when it comes.
For the LORD will be your confidence
and will keep your foot from being caught.

Proverbs 3:25-26

THE DEVIL WANTS TO REMIND YOU OF YOUR PAST TO CONVINCE YOU THAT YOU DESERVE YOUR PRESENT AND SHOULD BE FEARFUL OF YOUR FUTURE

For the LORD will be your confidence
and will keep your foot from being caught.

Proverbs 3:26

PEOPLE
KNOW
EVERYTHING
YOU
HAVE
BEEN

GOD
KNOWS
EVERYTHING
YOU
COULD
BE

◀◀   ▶▶

For the L ORD will be your confidence
and will keep your foot from being caught.

Proverbs 3:26

GREAT CONFIDENCE IS A
PREREQUISITE
FOR GREAT ACCOMPLISHMENT

The wise shall inherit glory,
but shame shall be the legacy of fools.

Proverbs 3:35

IF YOU DON'T
OWN YOUR PAST,
YOU UNDERMINE THE SUCCESS
OF YOUR FUTURE

FEBRUARY

1

Hear, my children, the instruction of a father,
and give attention to know understanding.
For I give you good doctrine.
Do not forsake my law.

Proverbs 4:1-2

The cost of discipline
is always high.
The cost of regret
is always higher.

Let your heart retain my words.
Keep my commands and live.

Proverbs 4:4b

Scripture isn't just something to memorize. It's something to obey.

Let your heart retain my words.
Keep my commands and live.
Proverbs 4:4b

YOU'LL NEVER GET THE
BEST OF GOD
IF YOU ONLY GIVE HIM
HALF OF YOU!

FEBRUARY

4

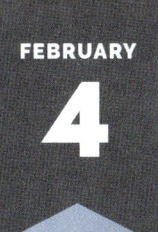

Get wisdom! Get understanding!
Do not forget, nor turn away from
the words of my mouth.
Do not forsake her,
and she will preserve you.
Love her, and she will keep you.

Proverbs 4:5-6

THERE IS A DIFFERENCE BETWEEN THE PERSON OF JESUS AND THE PRINCIPLES OF JESUS. IF YOU KNOW THE PERSON OF JESUS, YOU CAN BE ON YOUR WAY TO HEAVEN. BUT WITHOUT THE PRINCIPLES OF JESUS, YOU CAN EXPERIENCE HELL ON EARTH.

Wisdom is the principal thing,
therefore get wisdom.
And in all your getting, get understanding.
Proverbs 4:7

WISDOM IS
THE ABILITY TO
INTERPRET LIFE
THROUGH THE EYES OF GOD.

Exalt her, and she will promote you.
She will bring you honor
when you embrace her.

Proverbs 4:8

THE BEST YOU DID TODAY SHOULD BE THE FLOOR OF TOMORROW'S BETTER

Do not enter the path of the wicked,
and do not walk in the way of evil.
Avoid it, do not travel on it.
Turn away from it and pass on.

Proverbs 4:14-15

WHY RESIST TEMPTATION TOMORROW WHEN YOU CAN PREVENT IT TODAY?

Do not enter the path of the wicked,
and do not walk in the way of evil.
Avoid it, do not travel on it.
Turn away from it and pass on.

Proverbs 4:14-15

YOU CAN'T WIN FROM A LOSING POSITION.

But the path of the just
is like the shining sun
that shines ever brighter
unto the perfect day.
Proverbs 4:18

Always focus

on what

today could be

instead of what

yesterday was.

But the path of the just
is like the shining sun
that shines ever brighter
unto the perfect day.

Proverbs 4:18

You can't live your life
from there.
You must live your life
from here.

FEBRUARY

11

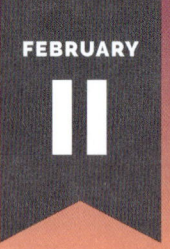

But the path of the just
is like the shining sun
that shines ever brighter
unto the perfect day.

Proverbs 4:18

You'll never find motivation in your rearview mirror.

FEBRUARY

12

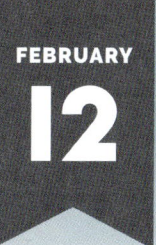

But the path of the just is like the shining sun that shines ever brighter unto the perfect day. The way of the wicked is like darkness. They do not know what makes them stumble.

Proverbs 4:18-19

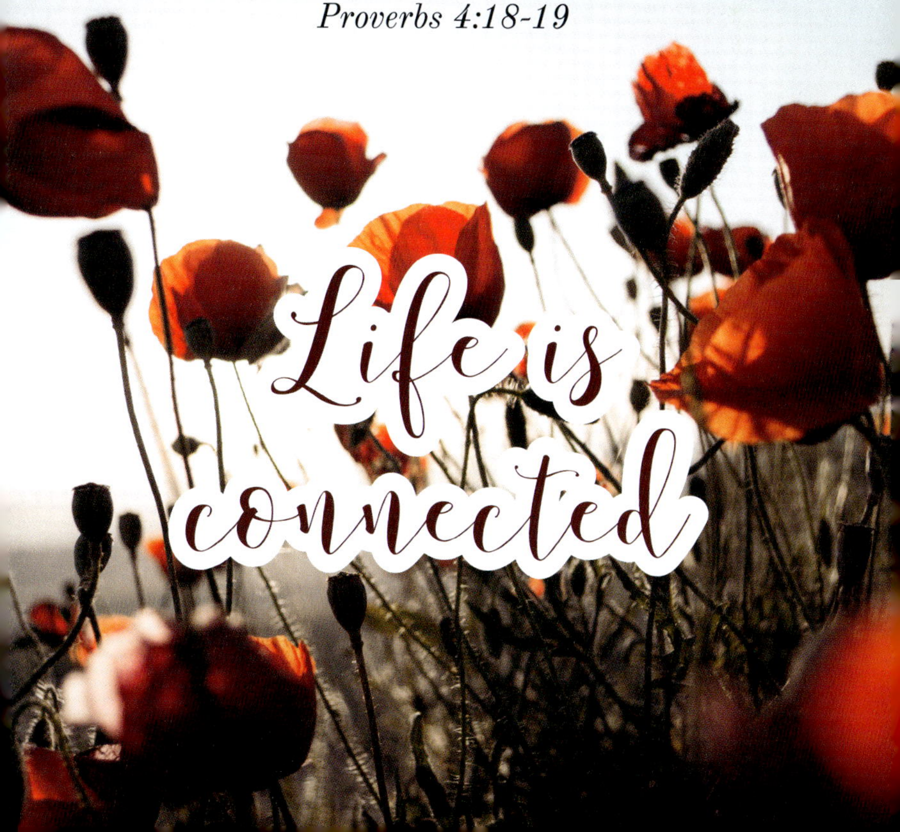
Life is connected

My son, give attention to my words.
Incline your ear to my sayings.
Proverbs 4:20

JUST BECAUSE
IT GETS YOUR ATTENTION
DOESN'T MEAN
IT DESERVES YOUR ATTENTION

FEBRUARY
14

My son, give attention to my words.
Incline your ear to my sayings.
Do not let them depart from your eyes.
Keep them in the midst of your heart.

Proverbs 4:20-21

You always have time
for what you *choose*
to have time for.

Keep your heart with all diligence,
for out of it spring the issues of life.

Proverbs 4:23

NEVER LET COMPLIMENTS GO TO YOUR HEAD. NEVER LET CRITICISM GO TO YOUR HEART.

Let your eyes look straight ahead
and your eyelids look right before you.

Proverbs 4:25

IF THE DEVIL CAN'T DESTROY YOU, HE'LL DISTRACT YOU. IF HE CAN DISTRACT YOU, THERE'S A GOOD CHANCE YOU'LL DESTROY YOURSELF.

Let your eyes look straight ahead
and your eyelids look right before you.
Proverbs 4:25

DOUBT GAINS POWER
WHEN YOU FOCUS ON THE
IRRELEVANT

Let your eyes look straight ahead
and your eyelids look right before you.
Proverbs 4:25

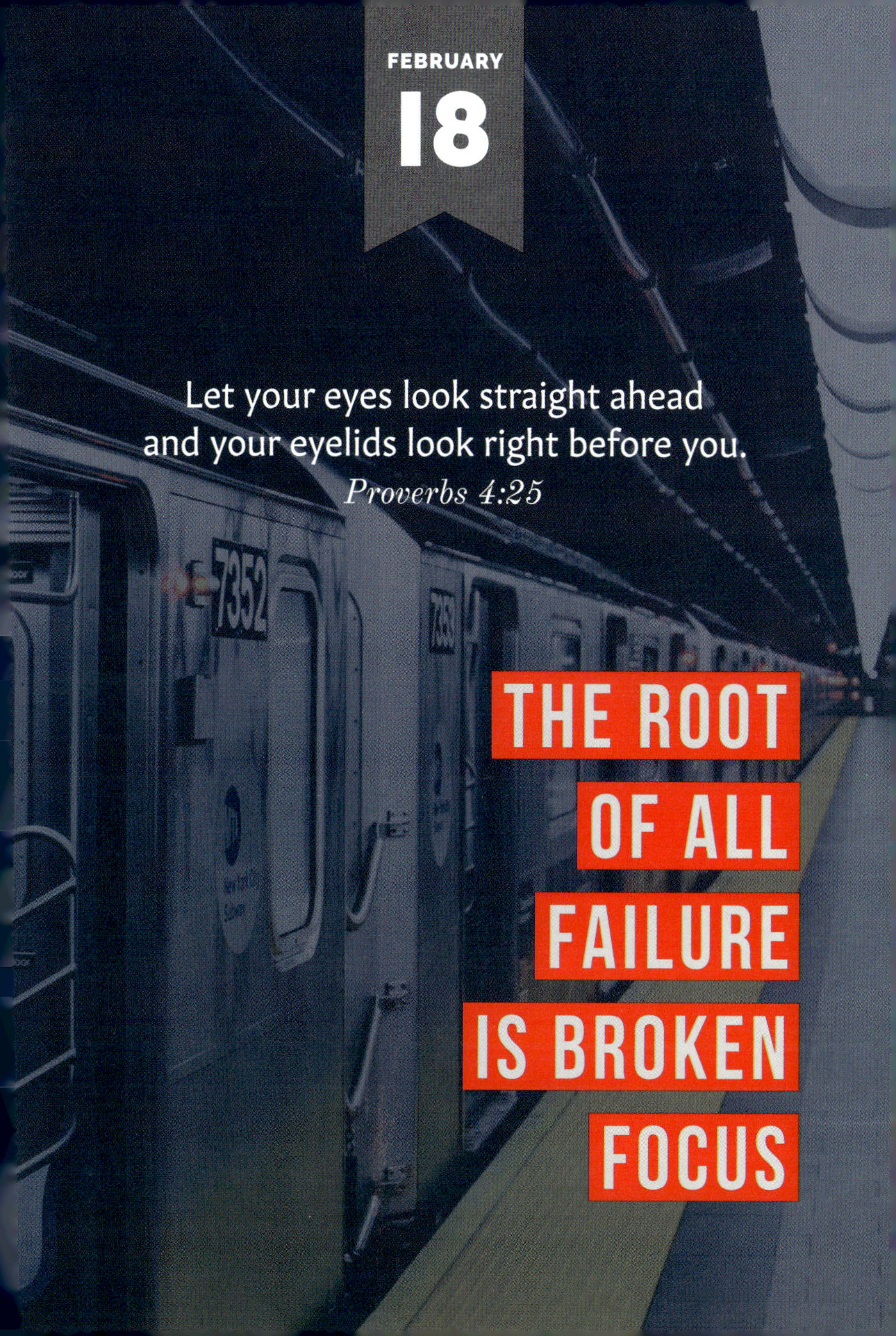

THE ROOT
OF ALL
FAILURE
IS BROKEN
FOCUS

FEBRUARY

19

Let your eyes look straight ahead
and your eyelids look right before you.

Proverbs 4:25

NEVER GAZE AT
WHAT YOU DON'T WANT
IN YOUR FUTURE

Ponder the path of your feet,
and let all your ways be established.

Proverbs 4:26

FAILURE COMES TO THOSE WHO THINK BUT NEVER DO, AS WELL AS TO THOSE WHO DO BUT NEVER THINK.

Do not turn to the right or the left.
Remove your foot from evil.

Proverbs 4:27

WHAT GETS YOUR ATTENTION GETS YOU!

That you may preserve discretion,
and your lips may keep knowledge.
For the lips of an immoral woman drip honey,
and her mouth is smoother than oil.
But in the end she is bitter as wormwood,
sharp as a two-edged sword.
Her feet go down to death.
Her steps lay hold of hell.

Proverbs 5:2-5

Failure occurs when you don't connect today's decisions with tomorrow's destiny.

Remove your way far from her,
and do not go near the door of her house,
lest you give your honor to others
and your years to the cruel one.

Proverbs 5:8-9

WHAT YOU CAN WALK AWAY FROM,
YOU HAVE MASTERED.
WHAT YOU CAN'T WALK AWAY FROM
HAS MASTERED YOU.

Drink water from your own cistern
and running water from your own well.

Proverbs 5:15

LEARN TO BE CONTENT WITH YOUR CONTENTS

FEBRUARY
25

Let your fountain be blessed,
and rejoice with the wife of your youth.
Proverbs 5:18

THE GRASS WILL ALWAYS
SEEM GREENER ON
THE OTHER SIDE...
UNTIL YOU HAVE TO
MOW IT.

His own iniquities entrap the wicked man,
and he is caught in the cords of his sin.

Proverbs 5:22

SIN IS
DECEPTIVE,
DESTRUCTIVE,
AND ADDICTIVE.

His own iniquities
entrap the wicked man,
and he is caught in the cords of his sin.

Proverbs 5:22

SIN WILL TAKE YOU
FURTHER THAN YOU WANT TO GO,
KEEP YOU LONGER THAN YOU WANT TO STAY,
AND COST YOU
MORE THAN YOU WANT TO PAY!

His own iniquities
entrap the wicked man,
and he is caught in the cords of his sin.
He shall die for lack of instruction,
and in the greatness of his folly
he shall go astray.

Proverbs 5:22-23

THE REBRANDING
OF SINS
MAKES THEM
MORE PALATABLE
BUT NO LESS
DEADLY

Go to the ant, you sluggard!
Consider her ways and be wise.
Which, having no captain, overseer, or ruler,
Provides her supplies in the summer
and gathers her food in the harvest.

Proverbs 6:6-8

DISCIPLINE IS SIMPLY CHOOSING BETWEEN WHAT YOU WANT NOW AND WHAT YOU WANT MOST.

My son, keep your father's command,
and do not forsake the law of your mother.
Bind them continually upon your heart.
Tie them around your neck.
When you roam, they will lead you.
When you sleep, they will keep you.
And when you awake, they will speak with you.

Proverbs 6:20-22

IN ORDER TO HEAR GOD'S VOICE, YOU MUST TURN DOWN THE VOLUME OF THE WORLD AND TURN UP THE VALUE OF THE WORD.

For the commandment is a lamp,
and the law a light.
Reproofs of instruction are the way of life,
to keep you from the evil woman,
from the flattering tongue of a seductress.

Proverbs 6:23-24

**THE REASON
GOD WON'T
LET YOU
GET AWAY
WITH SUCH
LOW DECISIONS
IS BECAUSE
YOU HAVE
SUCH A
HIGH CALLING**

Whoever commits adultery with a woman
lacks understanding.
He who does so destroys his own soul.
Proverbs 6:32

ADULTERY NEVER BEGINS
IN THE BED.
IT BEGINS IN THE HEAD.

MARCH

5

Passing along the street near her corner,
and he took the path to her house.
In the twilight, in the evening,
in the black and dark night.
And there a woman met him,
with the attire of a harlot and a crafty heart.

Proverbs 7:8-10

Sin grows best in the dark.

Now therefore, listen to me, my children.
Pay attention to the words of my mouth.
Do not let your heart turn aside to her ways.
Do not stray into her paths.
For she has cast down many wounded,
and all who were slain by her were strong men.
Her house is the way to hell,
descending to the chambers of death.

Proverbs 7:24-27

**Little compromises
that no one sees
produce great failures
that everyone sees.**

Listen, for I will speak of excellent things,
and from the opening of my lips
will come right things.

Proverbs 8:6

There is very little traffic ON THE EXTRA MILE.

Listen, for I will speak of excellent things,
and from the opening of my lips
will come right things.

Proverbs 8:6

YOU MUST BE WILLING TO DO THINGS POORLY BEFORE YOU CAN DO THEM EXCELLENTLY

Receive my instruction, and not silver,
and knowledge rather than choice gold.
For wisdom is better than rubies,
and all the things one may desire
cannot be compared with her.

Proverbs 8:10-11

LEARN TO LIVE FOR ETERNITY AND NOT JUST FOR THE WEEKEND.

I love those who love me,
and those who seek me diligently will find me.
Proverbs 8:17

If you prioritize the Word,
it will help you
prioritize your life.

When He prepared the heavens, I was there.
When He drew a circle on the face of the deep,
when He established the clouds above,
when He strengthened
the fountains of the deep,
when He assigned to the sea its limit,
so that the waters
would not transgress His command,
when He marked out
the foundations of the earth.

Proverbs 8:27-29

YOU CAN LIMIT A BIG GOD WITH YOUR SMALL THINKING

He who sins against me
wrongs his own soul.
All those who hate me love death.

Proverbs 8:36

Sin initially thrills but eventually kills.

Sin initially fascinates but eventually assassinates.

He who sins against me
wrongs his own soul.
All those who hate me love death.
Proverbs 8:36

YOU CAN'T DO WRONG THINGS AND GET RIGHT RESULTS.

He who corrects a scoffer
gets shame for himself,
and he who rebukes a wicked man
only harms himself.
Do not correct a scoffer, lest he hate you.
Rebuke a wise man, and he will love you.
Give instruction to a wise man,
and he will be still wiser.
Teach a just man,
and he will increase in learning.

Proverbs 9:7-9

Correct the simple and he won't understand you.
Correct the fool and he will ignore you.
Correct the scoffer and he will hate you.
Correct the wise and he will thank you.

Give instruction to a wise man,
and he will be still wiser.
Teach a just man,
and he will increase in learning.
Proverbs 9:9

THE MORE I KNOW,

THE MORE I KNOW

I NEED TO KNOW.

Give instruction to a wise man,
and he will be still wiser.
Teach a just man,
and he will increase in learning.

Proverbs 9:9

IN LIFE, YOU'RE EITHER WINNING OR LEARNING.

The fear of the LORD
is the beginning of wisdom,
and the knowledge of the Holy One
is understanding.

Proverbs 9:10

GO TO THE THRONE BEFORE YOU GO TO THE PHONE

The fear of the LORD
is the beginning of wisdom,
and the knowledge of the Holy One
is understanding.

Proverbs 9:10

WHATEVER YOU
PUT FIRST IN YOUR LIFE
WILL DETERMINE
YOUR DECISIONS

For by me your days will be multiplied,
and years of life will be added to you.

Proverbs 9:11

WHEN YOU RECOGNIZE THAT TOMORROW MATTERS, IT WILL CHANGE THE WAY YOU LIVE TODAY.

Stolen water is sweet,
and bread eaten in secret is pleasant.
But he does not know that the dead are there,
that her guests are in the depths of hell.

Proverbs 9:17-18

The forbidden is alluring, but the future it brings is alarming.

He who has a slack hand becomes poor,
but the hand of the diligent makes rich.

Proverbs 10:4

TENACITY
IS A NECESSITY
TO FULFILL
YOUR DESTINY

He who has a slack hand becomes poor,
but the hand of the diligent makes rich.
He who gathers in summer is a wise son.
He who sleeps in harvest
is a son who causes shame.

Proverbs 10:4-5

It's not a question
of whether or not
you will be busy.
The question is,
what will you
be busy doing?

MARCH

23

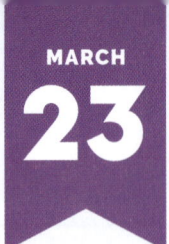

He who has a slack hand becomes poor,
but the hand of the diligent makes rich.
He who gathers in summer is a wise son.
He who sleeps in harvest
is a son who causes shame.

Proverbs 10:4-5

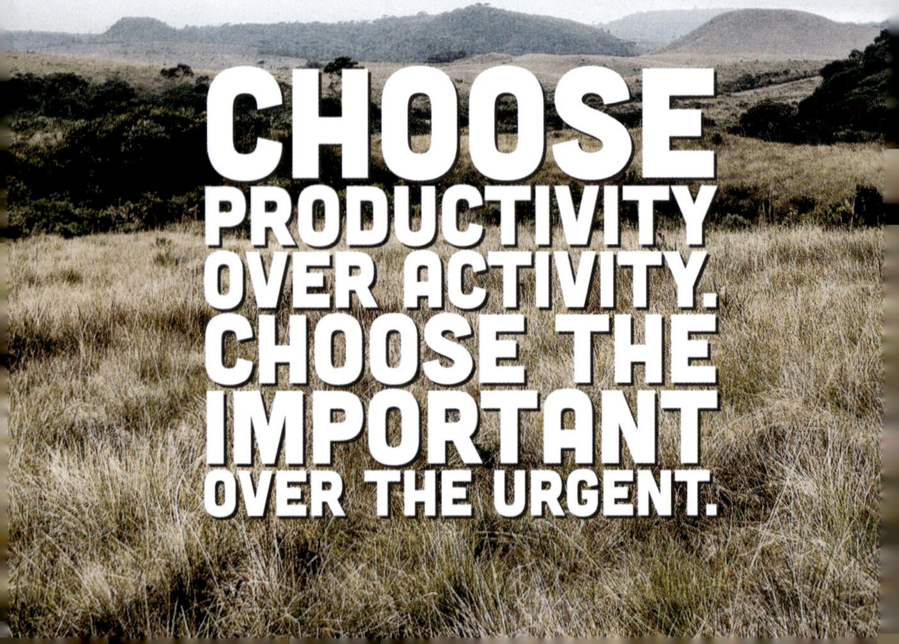
CHOOSE
PRODUCTIVITY
OVER ACTIVITY.
CHOOSE THE
IMPORTANT
OVER THE URGENT.

He who has a slack hand becomes poor,
but the hand of the diligent makes rich.
He who gathers in summer is a wise son.
He who sleeps in harvest
is a son who causes shame.

Proverbs 10:4-5

ALL PROCRASTINATION HAS ITS ROOT IN FEAR OR LAZINESS. TAKE AUTHORITY OVER IT!

He who walks with integrity walks securely,
but he who perverts his ways
will become known.

Proverbs 10:9

A CLEAR CONSCIENCE
MAKES FOR A SOFT
PILLOW

He who walks with integrity walks securely,
but he who perverts his ways
will become known.

Proverbs 10:9

THOSE WHO HAVE
NOTHING TO HIDE
HIDE NOTHING

MARCH
27

He who walks with integrity walks securely,
but he who perverts his ways
will become known.

Proverbs 10:9

WHAT YOU DO BY CANDLELIGHT
WILL DETERMINE WHO YOU WILL BE
IN THE SPOTLIGHT

He who walks with integrity walks securely,
but he who perverts his ways
will become known.

Proverbs 10:9

What you do
when no one is watching
determines who you will be
when everyone is watching.

He who keeps instruction is in the way of life,
but he who refuses correction goes astray.

Proverbs 10:17

DISCIPLINE
IS THE BRIDGE
BETWEEN GOALS AND
ACCOMPLISHMENTS

The blessing of the LORD makes one rich,
and He adds no sorrow with it.

Proverbs 10:22

IF THERE ARE
TOO MANY
SORROWS
IN THE BLESSING,
THE BLESSING DID
NOT COME
FROM GOD

The fear of the wicked will come upon him,
and the desire of the righteous will be granted.
Proverbs 10:24

IT'S OKAY TO
DESIRE MORE.
JUST DON'T FORGET
TO ENJOY THE NOW.

APRIL

1

As vinegar to the teeth and smoke to the eyes,
so is the lazy man to those who send him.
Proverbs 10:26

TRUST IS DEVELOPED
BY REPEATED BEHAVIOR.
CHARACTER
IS REVEALED
IN PRESSURE.

The fear of the LORD prolongs days,
but the years of the wicked
will be shortened.
Proverbs 10:27

EVERYONE KNOWS THEY ARE GOING TO EVENTUALLY DIE, BUT FEW ACTUALLY BELIEVE IT. IF WE DID, WE WOULD DO THINGS DIFFERENTLY TODAY.

The fear of the LORD prolongs days,
but the years of the wicked
will be shortened.

Proverbs 10:27

DON'T LIVE YOUR LIFE BY DEFAULT. LIVE YOUR LIFE BY DESIGN.

When pride comes, then comes shame.
But with the humble is wisdom.

Proverbs 11:2

DON'T THINK LESS OF YOURSELF. JUST THINK OF YOURSELF LESS

APRIL

5

The integrity of the upright
will guide them,
but the perversity of the unfaithful
will destroy them.

Proverbs 11:3

INTEGRITY CHOOSES
PEOPLE OVER THINGS,
PRINCIPLE OVER CONVENIENCE,
DISCRETION OVER IMMEDIACY,
AND CHARACTER
OVER PERSONAL GAIN.

The integrity of the upright
will guide them,
but the perversity of the unfaithful
will destroy them.

Proverbs 11:3

TRUST IS THE FOUNDATION
OF ALL RELATIONSHIPS

The integrity of the upright
will guide them,
but the perversity of the unfaithful
will destroy them.

Proverbs 11:3

INTEGRITY IS EASY
AS LONG AS IT
COSTS YOU NOTHING

The integrity of the upright
will guide them,
but the perversity of the unfaithful
will destroy them.

Proverbs 11:3

Never make decisions
just because they are easy.
Never make decisions
just because they are cheap.
Never make decisions
just because they are popular.
Make decisions
because they are right.

The integrity of the upright
will guide them,
but the perversity of the unfaithful
will destroy them.

Proverbs 11:3

REAL CHAMPIONS
ARE NOT DETERMINED
BY WHAT THEY DO
WHEN PEOPLE ARE WATCHING
BUT THE LIFE THEY LIVE
WHEN NO ONE IS WATCHING

APRIL

10

A talebearer reveals secrets,
but he who is of a faithful spirit
conceals a matter.

Proverbs 11:13

NEVER

TELL

YOUR

PROBLEMS

TO SOMEONE

WHO CAN'T

SOLVE THEM

APRIL

11

A talebearer reveals secrets,
but he who is of a faithful spirit
conceals a matter.

Proverbs 11:13

PEOPLE CEASE TO
FOLLOW
THOSE THEY
CANNOT TRUST

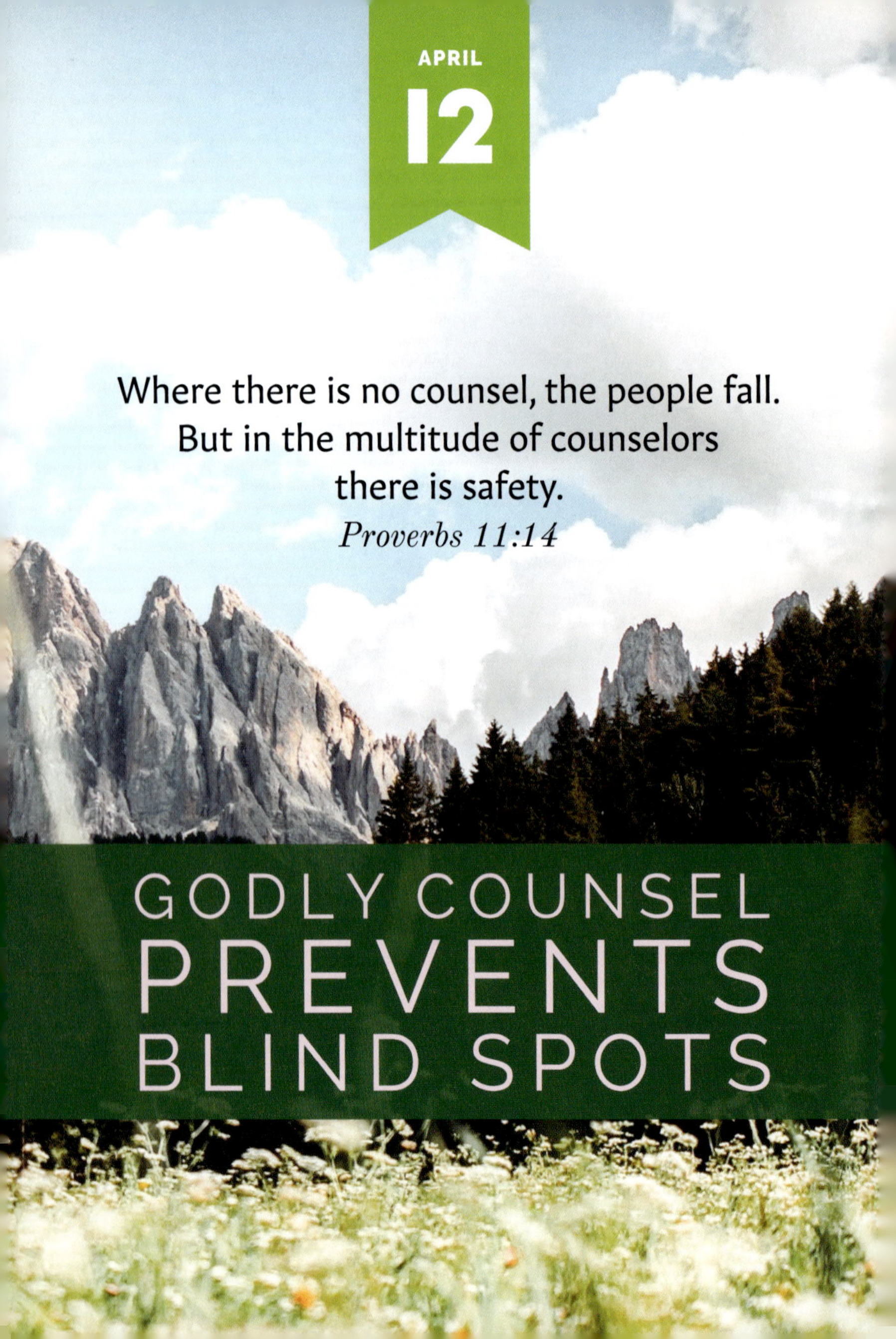

APRIL

12

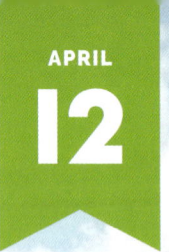

Where there is no counsel, the people fall.
But in the multitude of counselors
there is safety.

Proverbs 11:14

GODLY COUNSEL PREVENTS BLIND SPOTS

APRIL

13

There is one who scatters,
yet increases more.
And there is one who withholds
more than is right,
but it leads to poverty.

Proverbs 11:24

BE A GENEROUS GIVER, A CONSERVATIVE SPENDER, AND A WISE STEWARD.

There is one who scatters,
yet increases more.
And there is one who
withholds more than is right,
but it leads to poverty.
Proverbs 11:24

**LIFE IS NOT ABOUT
COVETOUS LIVING.
LIFE IS ABOUT
COVENANT GIVING.**

There is one who scatters,
yet increases more.
And there is one who
withholds more than is right,
but it leads to poverty.
Proverbs 11:24

Taking reveals
your selfishness.
Receiving rewards
your humility.
Giving reflects
your love.

APRIL
16

The generous soul will be made rich,
and he who waters
will also be watered himself.

Proverbs 11:25

Contentment causes you
to enjoy today.
Desire causes you
to expect a better tomorrow.

The generous soul will be made rich,
and he who waters
will also be watered himself.

Proverbs 11:25

THE VALUE OF YOUR LIFE
IS NOT DETERMINED BY
HOW MUCH YOU ACCUMULATE.
THE VALUE OF YOUR LIFE
IS DETERMINED BY
HOW MUCH YOU GIVE AWAY.

The people will curse him
who withholds grain,
but blessing will be on the head
of him who sells it.

Proverbs 11:26

WHATEVER
YOU HOLD BACK FROM GOD
WILL EVENTUALLY BE A MESS

WHATEVER
YOU GIVE TO GOD
WILL EVENTUALLY BE BLESSED

APRIL

19

The fruit of the righteous is a tree of life,
and he who wins souls is wise.

Proverbs 11:30

*The only things
that last forever
are people.*

The fruit of the righteous is a tree of life,
and he who wins souls is wise.

Proverbs 11:30

Good works don't win points with God.

— — —

Good works win souls for God.

The fruit of the righteous is a tree of life, and he who wins souls is wise.

Proverbs 11:30

YOU ARE *NOT* SAVED *BY* GOOD WORKS.

YOU ARE SAVED *FOR* GOOD WORKS.

The fruit of the righteous is a tree of life, and he who wins souls is wise.

Proverbs 11:30

SAVED PEOPLE SERVE PEOPLE

A man is not established by wickedness,
but the root of the righteous
cannot be moved.

Proverbs 12:3

**YOU MAY NOT KNOW WHERE
THE STORM STARTED
OR WHY IT STARTED,
BUT YOU CAN REST YOUR HEAD
ON THE PROMISES OF GOD
BECAUSE YOU'RE
GOING TO THE OTHER SIDE!**

The wicked are overthrown and are no more,
but the house of the righteous will stand.

Proverbs 12:7

HAVING PROBLEMS DOESN'T MAKE YOU SPECIAL. CHOOSING TO FACE AND OVERCOME THEM DOES!

APRIL

25

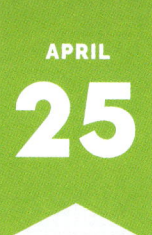

A man will be commended
according to his wisdom,
but he who is of a perverse heart
will be despised.

Proverbs 12:8

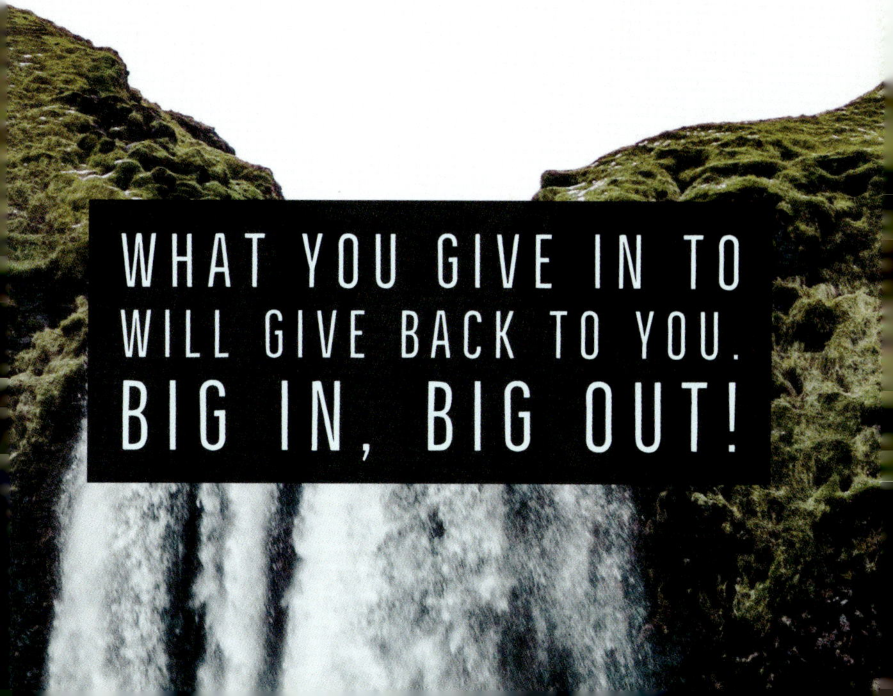

**WHAT YOU GIVE IN TO
WILL GIVE BACK TO YOU.
BIG IN, BIG OUT!**

He who tills his land
will be satisfied with bread,
but he who follows frivolity
is devoid of understanding.

Proverbs 12:11

There is no success
without *sacrifice.*

The wicked is ensnared
by the transgression of his lips,
but the righteous will come through trouble.

Proverbs 12:13

**JUST KEEP DRIVING.
STORMS WILL
ALWAYS
END UP IN YOUR
REARVIEW MIRROR**

The wicked is ensnared
by the transgression of his lips,
but the righteous will come through trouble.

Proverbs 12:13

PAIN WAS NEVER MEANT
TO BE A PLACE OF
PERMANENCE

The wicked is ensnared
by the transgression of his lips,
but the righteous will come through trouble.

Proverbs 12:13

IF YOU LOOK AT YOUR PROBLEM AS SPECIAL, IT WILL BE ESPECIALLY HARD TO OVERCOME

The way of a fool
is right in his own eyes,
but he who heeds counsel is wise.

Proverbs 12:15

ANY COUNSEL THAT GIVES YOU PERMISSION TO SELF-DESTRUCT IS NOT GODLY COUNSEL

There is one who speaks
like the piercings of a sword,
but the tongue of the wise
promotes health.

Proverbs 12:18

PEOPLE HEAR YOUR

WORDS

BUT THEY

FEEL YOUR

ATTITUDE

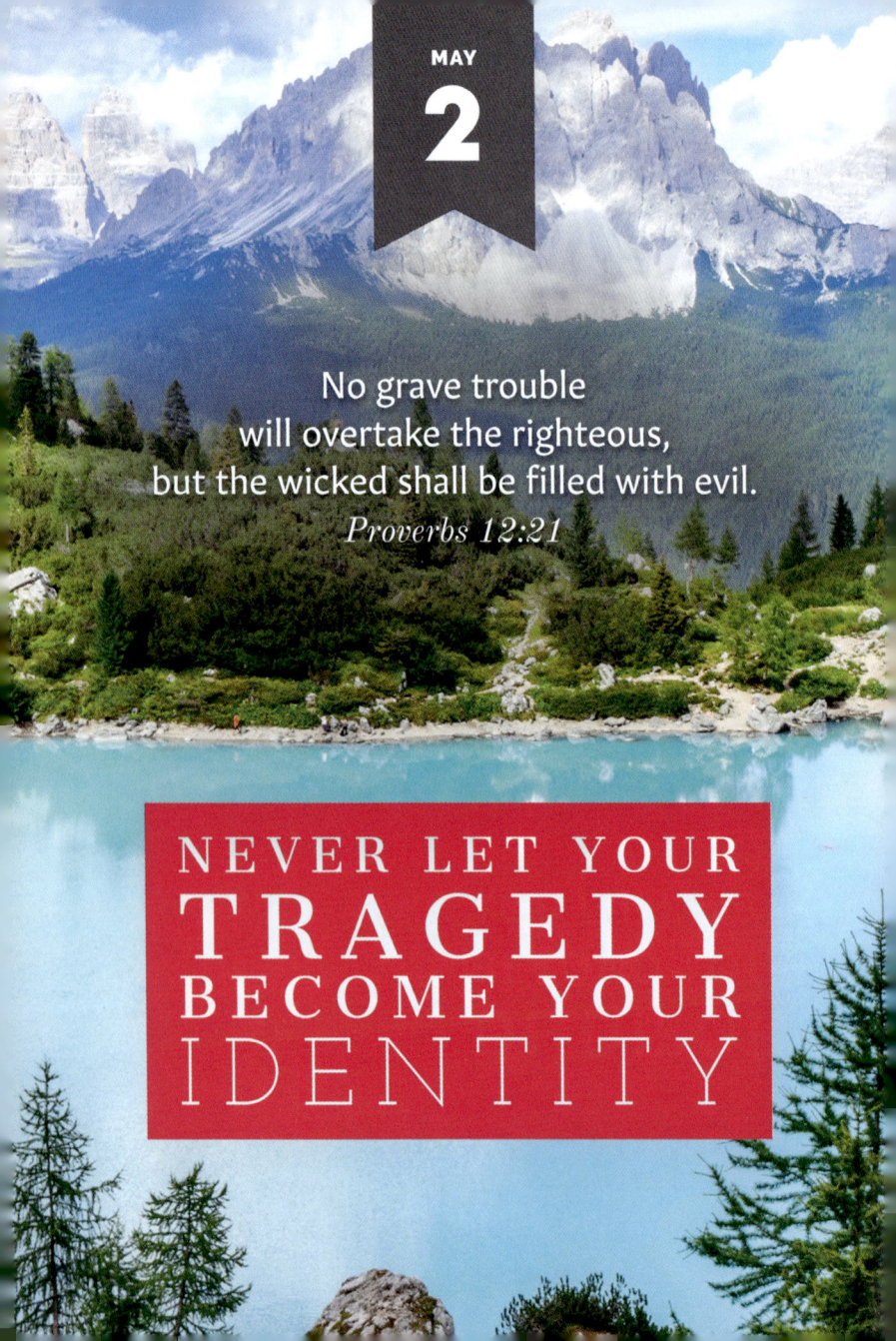

MAY

2

No grave trouble
will overtake the righteous,
but the wicked shall be filled with evil.
Proverbs 12:21

NEVER LET YOUR
TRAGEDY
BECOME YOUR
IDENTITY

MAY
3

The hand of the diligent will rule,
but the lazy man will be put to forced labor.

Proverbs 12:24

EVERYTHING
YIELDS TO DILIGENCE.

Anxiety in the heart of man causes depression,
but a good word makes it glad.

Proverbs 12:25

ENCOURAGEMENT
IS OXYGEN
TO THE SOUL

The righteous
should choose his friends carefully,
for the way of the wicked leads them astray.
Proverbs 12:26

SOME RELATIONSHIPS NEED TO BE

INITIATED

SOME RELATIONSHIPS NEED TO BE

CULTIVATED

SOME RELATIONSHIPS NEED TO BE

ELIMINATED

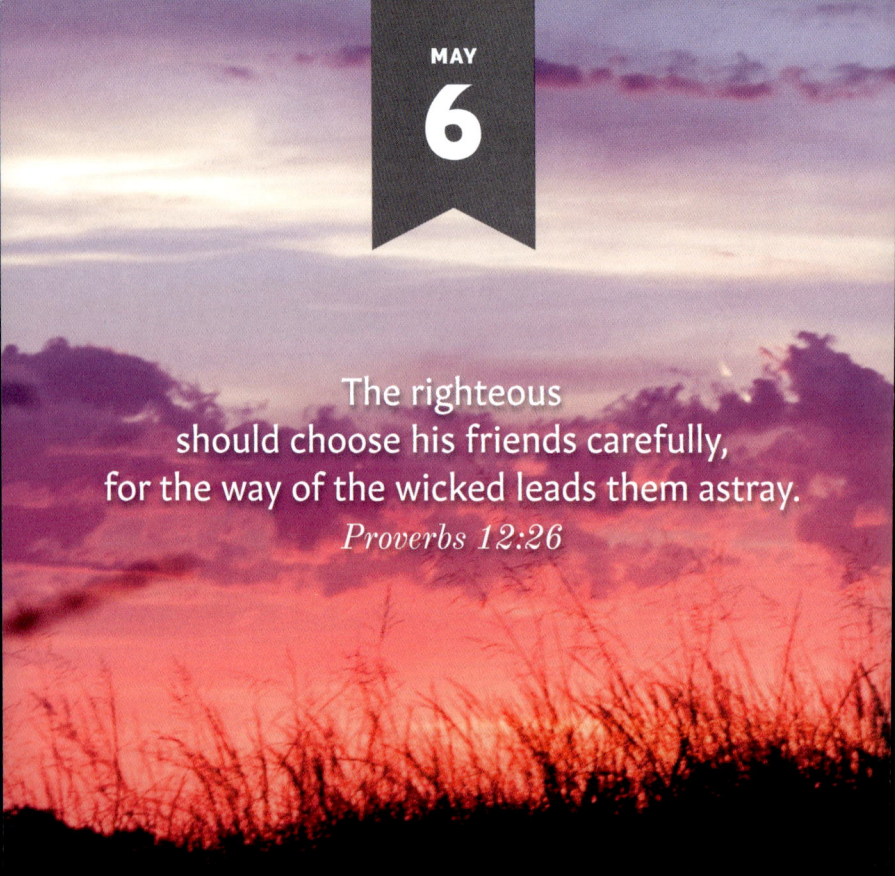

MAY
6

The righteous
should choose his friends carefully,
for the way of the wicked leads them astray.
Proverbs 12:26

*Your weakest friend
is the devil's strongest
entry point.*

MAY

7

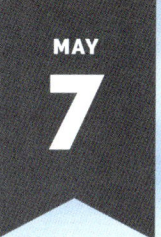

The righteous
should choose his friends carefully,
for the way of the wicked leads them astray.

Proverbs 12:26

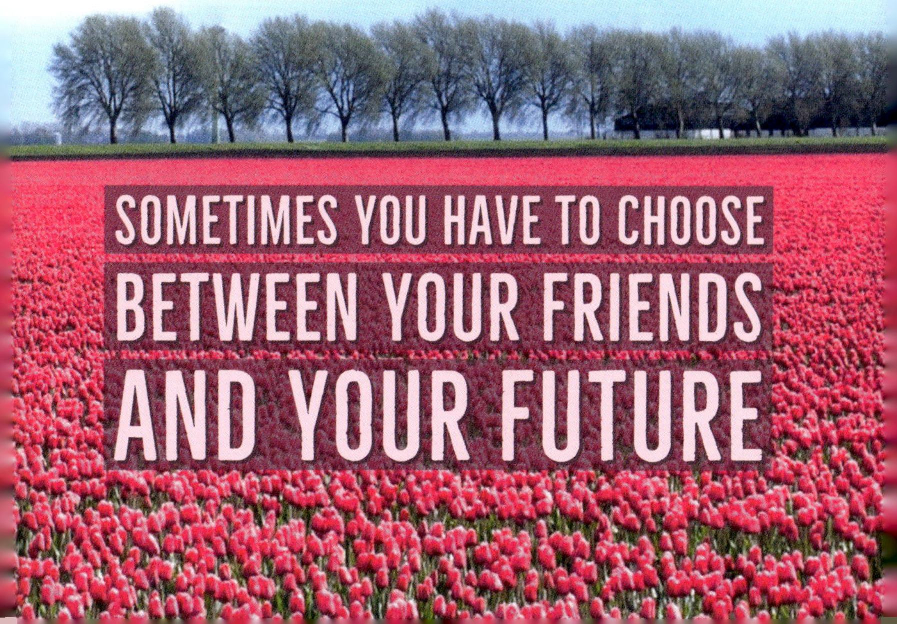
SOMETIMES YOU HAVE TO CHOOSE
BETWEEN YOUR FRIENDS
AND YOUR FUTURE

MAY

8

The righteous
should choose his friends carefully,
for the way of the wicked leads them astray.
Proverbs 12:26

THERE ARE TWO KINDS OF PEOPLE IN LIFE:
THOSE WHO LOVE WHERE YOU'VE BEEN
**AND THOSE WHO LOVE
WHERE YOU'RE GOING**

The righteous
should choose his friends carefully,
for the way of the wicked leads them astray.

Proverbs 12:26

SURROUND YOURSELF WITH PEOPLE WHO HELP YOU SEE YOUR OBJECTIVES, NOT YOUR OBSTACLES.

The soul of a lazy man
desires and has nothing,
but the soul of the diligent
shall be made rich.

Proverbs 13:4

LITTLE SACRIFICES
THAT NO ONE SEES
PRODUCE GREAT RESULTS
THAT EVERYONE WANTS

The soul of a lazy man
desires and has nothing,
but the soul of the diligent
shall be made rich.

Proverbs 13:4

SUCCESS IS SIMPLY ACCOMPLISHING

WHAT YOU WERE CREATED TO DO

The soul of a lazy man
desires and has nothing,
but the soul of the diligent
shall be made rich.
Proverbs 13:4

YOU CAN'T HAVE UPHILL HOPES AND DOWNHILL HABITS

The soul of a lazy man
desires and has nothing,
but the soul of the diligent
shall be made rich.

Proverbs 13:4

It's easy to want
the results of change
without being willing to pay
the price of change.

Wealth gained by dishonesty will be diminished, but he who gathers by labor will increase.

Proverbs 13:11

IF YOU THINK ABOUT BIG THINGS WHEN YOU ARE DOING SMALL THINGS, THE SMALL THINGS BECOME MEANINGFUL THINGS.

MAY
15

Hope deferred makes the heart sick,
but when the desire comes, it is a tree of life.
Proverbs 13:12

TIRED EYES
NEVER SEE
A BRIGHT FUTURE

Hope deferred makes the heart sick,
but when the desire comes, it is a tree of life.
Proverbs 13:12

**CHAMPIONS
ARE SIMPLY
THOSE WHO
PUT THEIR
GOD-GIVEN
DREAMS
ABOVE THEIR
MAN-MADE
FEARS**

The law of the wise is a fountain of life,
to turn one away from the snares of death.
Proverbs 13:14

CHARACTER IS WINNING THE BATTLE BETWEEN WHAT YOU WANT TO DO AND WHAT YOU SHOULD DO

Good understanding gains favor,
but the way of the unfaithful is hard.

Proverbs 13:15

YOU WILL NEVER PROGRESS BEYOND YOUR LAST POINT OF DISOBEDIENCE.

He who walks with wise men will be wise,
but the companion of fools
will be destroyed.
Proverbs 13:20

**DON'T LET THE
ENVIRONMENT
INFLUENCE YOUR
ENTHUSIASM**

**LET YOUR
ENTHUSIASM
DETERMINE YOUR
ENVIRONMENT**

MAY

20

He who walks with wise men will be wise,
but the companion of fools
will be destroyed.
Proverbs 13:20

YOU CAN'T HAVE

NEGATIVE FRIENDS

AND LIVE A

POSITIVE LIFE

He who walks with wise men will be wise,
but the companion of fools
will be destroyed.

Proverbs 13:20

A GOOD LEADER, WHEN HE GETS THE CHANCE, MAKES A FRIEND.

MAY
22

He who walks with wise men will be wise,
but the companion of fools
will be destroyed.
Proverbs 13:20

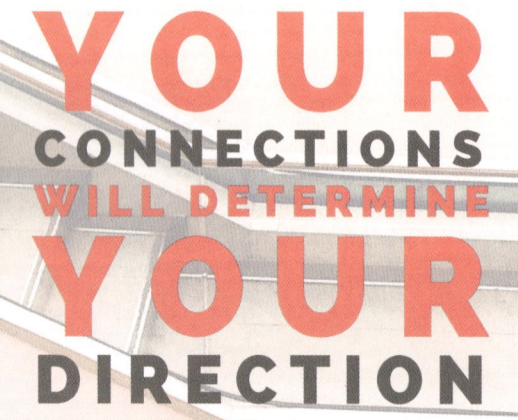

YOUR
CONNECTIONS
WILL DETERMINE
YOUR
DIRECTION

He who walks with wise men will be wise,
but the companion of fools
will be destroyed.

Proverbs 13:20

THE VOICES
YOU HEAR
DETERMINE
THE CHOICES
YOU MAKE

The heart knows its own bitterness,
and a stranger does not share its joy.

Proverbs 14:10

*Walk through
crowds slowly.
The smile on a face
may be masking
the hurt in a heart.*

MAY
25

The house of the wicked
will be overthrown,
but the tent of the upright will flourish.

Proverbs 14:11

Don't tell people
how bad they are.
Show them how good God is!

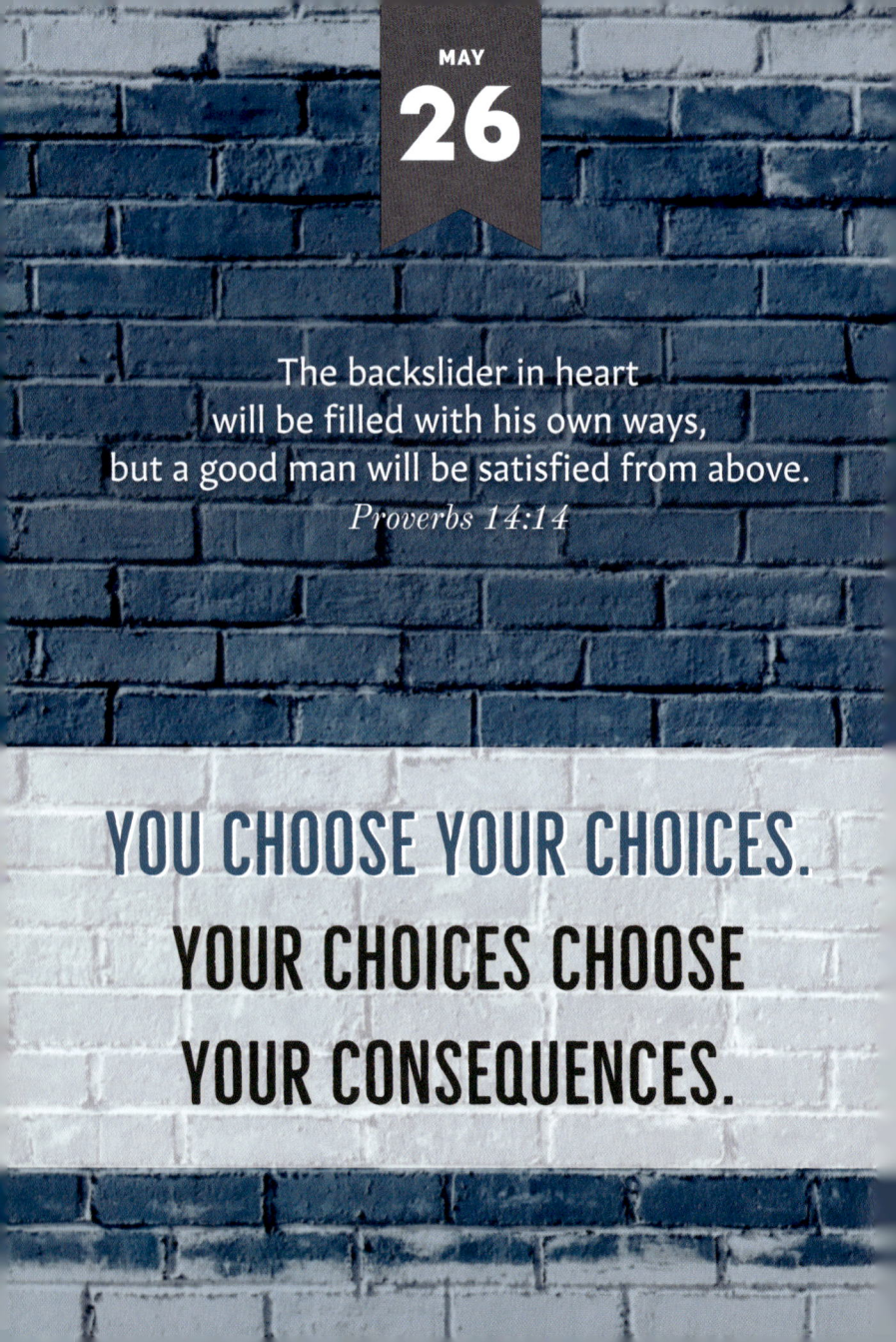

MAY

26

The backslider in heart
will be filled with his own ways,
but a good man will be satisfied from above.
Proverbs 14:14

YOU CHOOSE YOUR CHOICES.

YOUR CHOICES CHOOSE YOUR CONSEQUENCES.

MAY

27

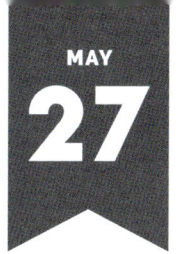

The backslider in heart
will be filled with his own ways,
but a good man will be satisfied from above.

Proverbs 14:14

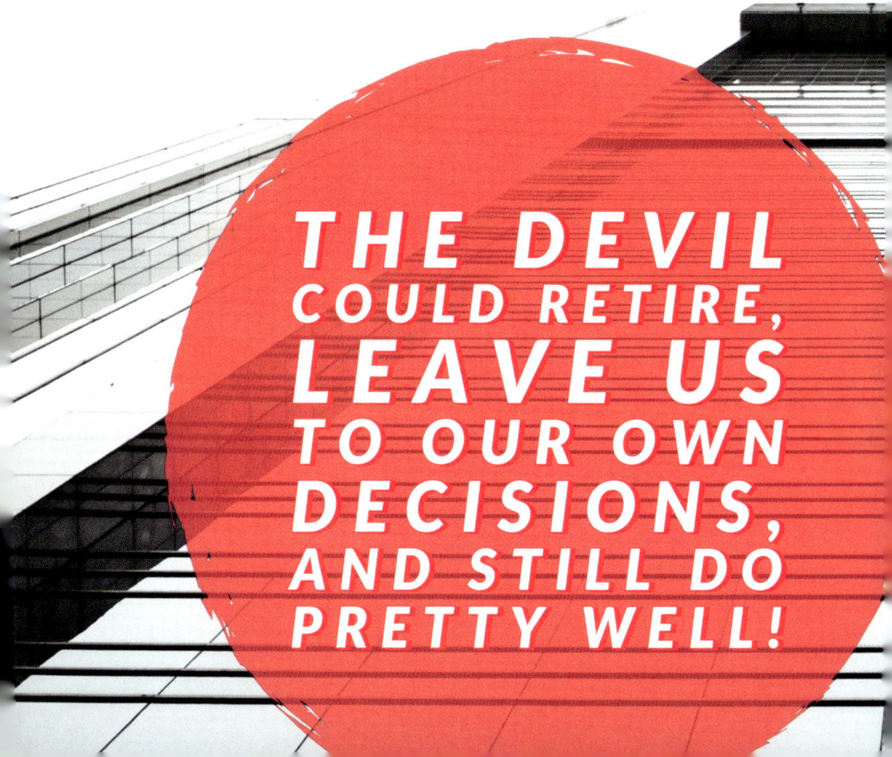
THE DEVIL
COULD RETIRE,
LEAVE US
TO OUR OWN
DECISIONS,
AND STILL DO
PRETTY WELL!

The simple inherit folly,
but the prudent are crowned with knowledge.

Proverbs 14:18

DON'T BE CYNICAL, BUT DON'T BE GULLIBLE.

In all labor there is profit,
but idle chatter leads only to poverty.

Proverbs 14:23

QUIT ASKING FOR

MORE

WHEN YOU

HAVEN'T MASTERED

LESS

In all labor there is profit,
but idle chatter leads only to poverty.

Proverbs 14:23

FINISHERS ARE SIMPLY ORDINARY PEOPLE WITH EXTRAORDINARY DETERMINATION

The crown of the wise is their riches,
but the foolishness of fools is folly.

Proverbs 14:24

ALWAYS DO
WHAT'S RIGHT
BEFORE YOU
DO WHAT'S FUN,
UNLESS DOING
WHAT'S FUN
IS RIGHT!

The crown of the wise is their riches,
but the foolishness of fools is folly.

Proverbs 14:24

**Money
doesn't
create
character.
It reveals it.**

The crown of the wise is their riches,
but the foolishness of fools is folly.
Proverbs 14:24

MONEY CREATES OPTIONS.
HOW YOU HANDLE THE OPTIONS
REVEALS YOUR CHARACTER.

A wholesome tongue is a tree of life,
but perverseness in it breaks the spirit.

Proverbs 15:4

**Everything you say
needs to be true.
But not everything that is true
needs to be said.**

The sacrifice of the wicked
is an abomination to the LORD,
but the prayer of the upright is His delight.

Proverbs 15:8

Let God's Word be His part
of your prayer life.
When you do, you pray the answer
and not the problem.

A merry heart makes a cheerful countenance,
but by sorrow of the heart the spirit is broken.
Proverbs 15:13

YOU CAN'T BE

DEFEATED

IF YOU CAN'T BE

DISCOURAGED

A merry heart makes a cheerful countenance,
but by sorrow of the heart the spirit is broken.

Proverbs 15:13

NEVER PLACE YOUR EMOTIONAL WELL-BEING IN THE HANDS OF ANOTHER

All the days of the afflicted are evil,
but he who is of a merry heart
has a continual feast.

Proverbs 15:15

BLESSED ARE THOSE
WHO CAN LAUGH AT THEMSELVES,
FOR THEY SHALL NEVER
CEASE TO BE ENTERTAINED!

All the days of the afflicted are evil,
but he who is of a merry heart
has a continual feast.

Proverbs 15:15

*A PERSON WHO THINKS
THEY NEED SUNSHINE
TO BE HAPPY
HAS CLEARLY NEVER
DANCED IN THE RAIN*

All the days of the afflicted are evil,
but he who is of a merry heart
has a continual feast.

Proverbs 15:15

YOU'LL NEVER GET A
SECOND CHANCE
TO ENJOY
YOUR TODAY

JUNE

10

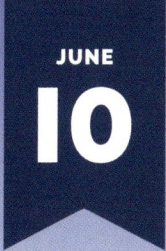

Better is a little with the fear of the LORD
than great treasure with trouble.

Proverbs 15:16

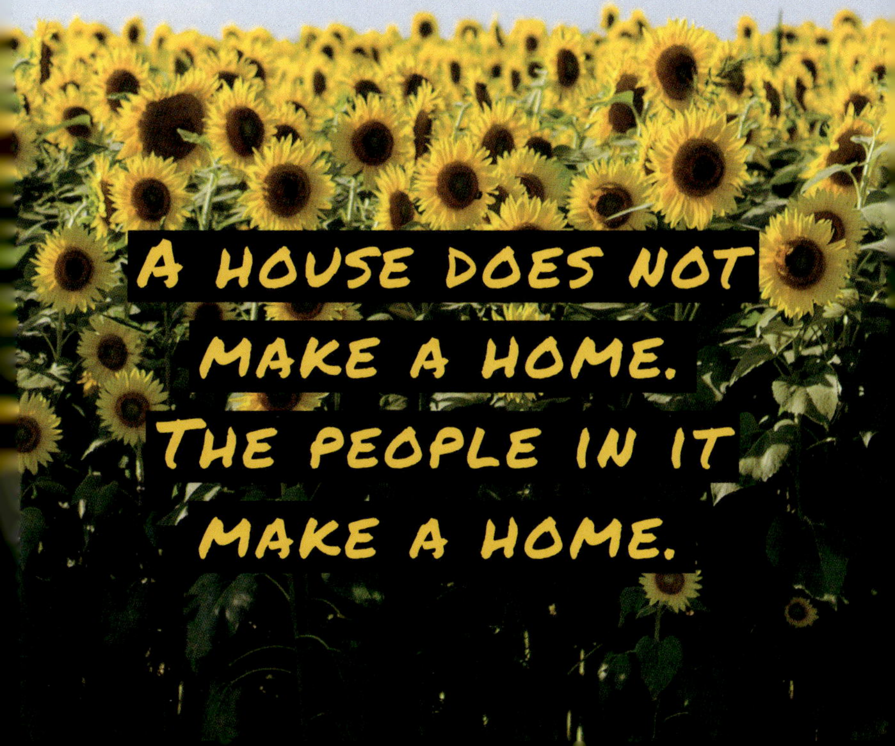

A HOUSE DOES NOT
MAKE A HOME.
THE PEOPLE IN IT
MAKE A HOME.

JUNE

II

Better is a dinner of herbs where love is than a fatted calf with hatred.

Proverbs 15:17

THE QUALITY OF YOUR LIFE IS NOT DETERMINED BY THE QUANTITY OF *WHAT YOU HAVE*

The way of the lazy man
is like a hedge of thorns,
but the way of the upright is a highway.
Proverbs 15:19

IT'S NOT THE SIN YOU STRUGGLE WITH THAT WILL KILL YOU. IT'S THE SIN YOU TOLERATE

A man has joy by the answer of his mouth,
and a word spoken in due season,
how good it is!

Proverbs 15:23

*DON'T SAVE FLOWERS
FOR FUNERALS.
GIVE EULOGIES TO THE LIVING.*

The way of life winds upward for the wise,
that he may turn away from hell below.

Proverbs 15:24

TO FOSTER A BETTER FUTURE,
YOU MUST BECOME
DISSATISFIED
WITH THE PRESENT

The way of life winds upward for the wise,
that he may turn away from hell below.

Proverbs 15:24

REALITY IS WHERE YOU STAND.
VISION IS WHERE
YOU SOAR

The heart of the righteous studies how to answer,
but the mouth of the wicked pours forth evil.

Proverbs 15:28

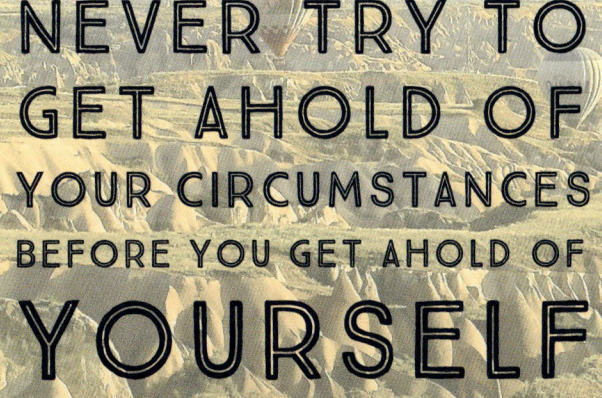

NEVER TRY TO
GET AHOLD OF
YOUR CIRCUMSTANCES
BEFORE YOU GET AHOLD OF
YOURSELF

The heart of the righteous studies how to answer,
but the mouth of the wicked pours forth evil.

Proverbs 15:28

DON'T GIVE ANSWERS OFF THE TOP OF YOUR HEAD.
GIVE ANSWERS FROM THE BOTTOM OF YOUR HEART.

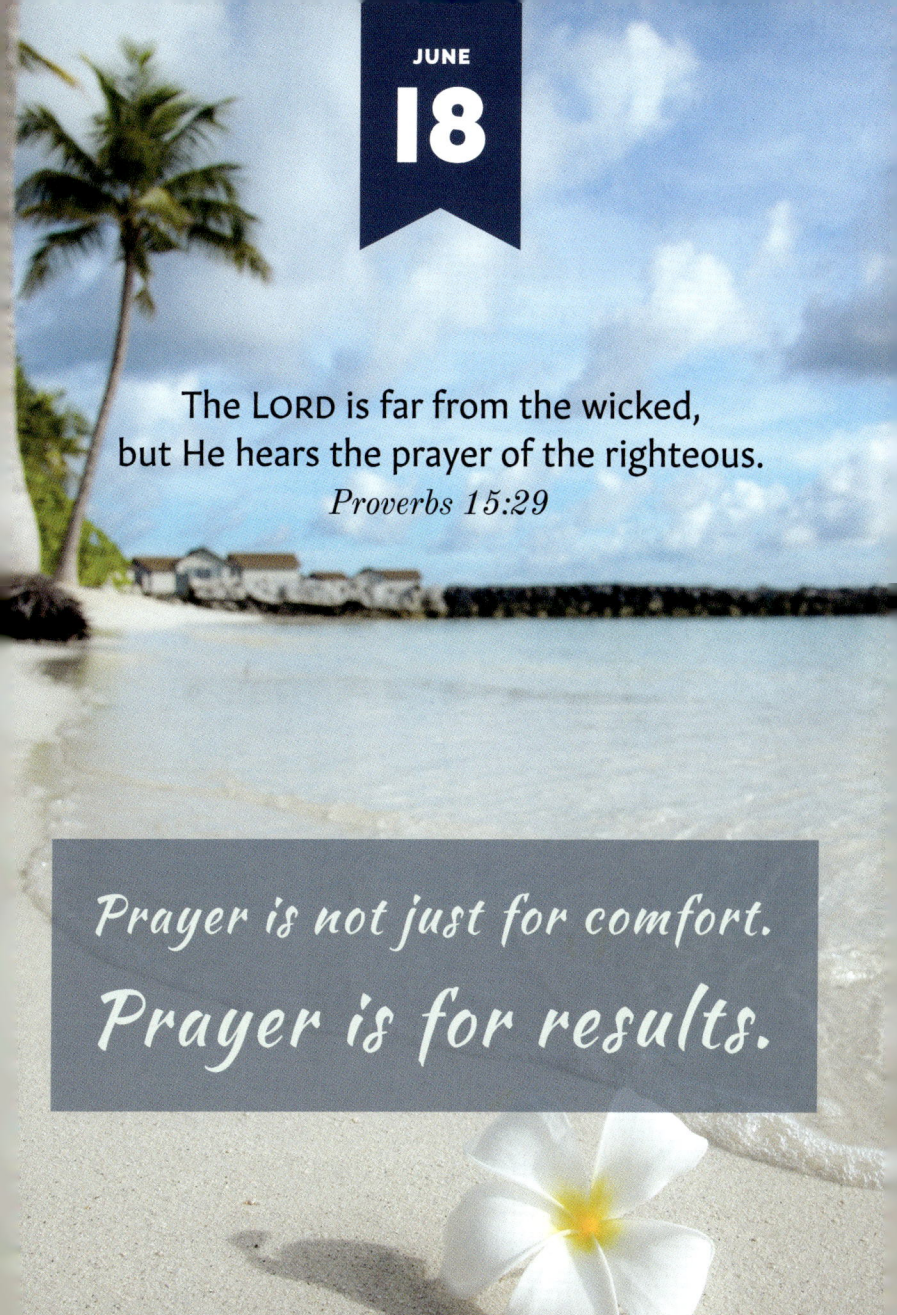

The LORD is far from the wicked,
but He hears the prayer of the righteous.
Proverbs 15:29

Prayer is not just for comfort.
Prayer is for results.

JUNE

19

The fear of the LORD
is the instruction of wisdom,
and before honor is humility.

Proverbs 15:33

HOW YOU PERCEIVE SOMEONE IS HOW YOU RECEIVE SOMEONE

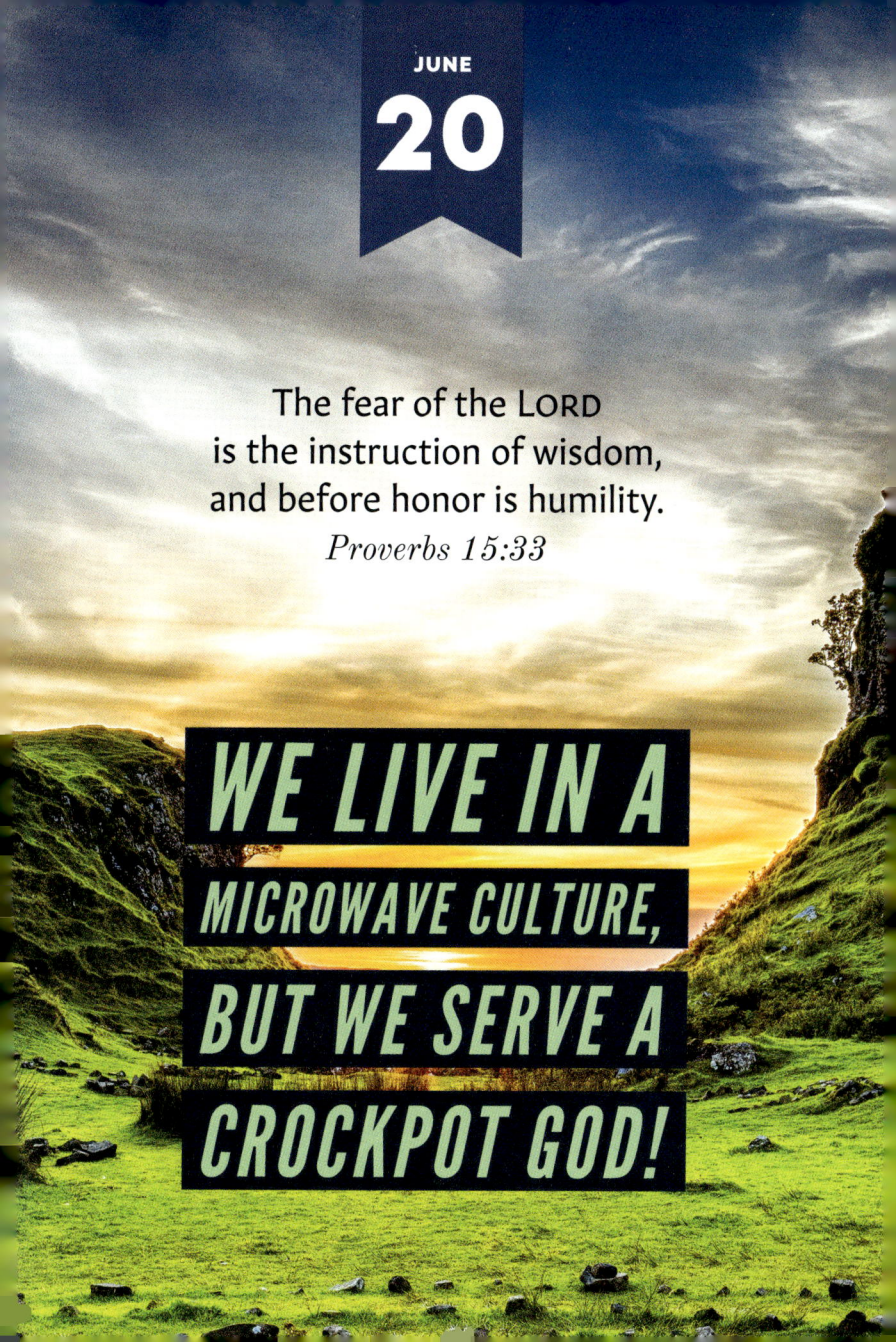

JUNE

20

The fear of the LORD
is the instruction of wisdom,
and before honor is humility.

Proverbs 15:33

WE LIVE IN A MICROWAVE CULTURE, BUT WE SERVE A CROCKPOT GOD!

All the ways of a man
are pure in his own eyes,
but the LORD
weighs the spirits.

Proverbs 16:2

IF YOU ARE DRIVEN BY THE RIGHT "WHY," GOD WILL LEAD YOU TO THE RIGHT "WHAT"

Commit your works to the LORD,
and your thoughts will be established.

Proverbs 16:3

LIFE IS LIKE A ROLL OF TOILET PAPER. THE CLOSER YOU GET TO THE END, THE FASTER IT GOES!

In mercy and truth,
atonement is provided for iniquity,
and by the fear of the LORD
one departs from evil.

Proverbs 16:6

FAILURE IS AN EVENT, NOT YOUR IDENTITY.

In mercy and truth,
atonement is provided for iniquity,
and by the fear of the LORD
one departs from evil.

Proverbs 16:6

NEVER LET WHAT YOU DID DEFINE YOU. ALWAYS LET WHAT JESUS CHRIST HAS DONE FOR YOU DEFINE YOU!

A man's heart plans his way,
but the LORD directs his steps.
Proverbs 16:9

YOU CAME FOR "THIS," BUT GOD HAS A "THAT." GOD'S "THAT" IS ALWAYS BETTER THAN YOUR "THIS."

A man's heart plans his way,
but the LORD directs his steps.

Proverbs 16:9

IF YOU ARE FAITHFUL "HERE," RIGHT WHERE YOU ARE, GOD WILL LEAD YOU TO A MUCH BETTER "THERE."

A man's heart plans his way,
but the LORD directs his steps.

Proverbs 16:9

LIFE IS A JOURNEY.
FOCUS ON THE LITTLE THINGS
THAT MAKE IT MORE
ENJOYABLE

A man's heart plans his way,
but the LORD directs his steps.

Proverbs 16:9

YOU CAN GET ANYWHERE YOU WANT
TO GO AS LONG AS YOU ARE WILLING
TO TAKE ENOUGH SMALL STEPS.

JUNE

29

Understanding is a wellspring of life
to him who has it,
but the correction of fools is folly.

Proverbs 16:22

A FOOL IS NOT
MENTALLY DEFICIENT.
A FOOL IS SELF-SUFFICIENT.

The heart of the wise teaches his mouth
and adds learning to his lips.
Proverbs 16:23

GIVE YOUR MOUTH
TIME TO CATCH UP
WITH YOUR HEART.

The person who labors,
labors for himself,
for his hungry mouth drives him on.

Proverbs 16:26

Limitations breed innovation.

An ungodly man digs up evil,
and it is on his lips like a burning fire.

Proverbs 16:27

LEARN TO BE A PROBLEM SOLVER, NOT A PROBLEM POINTER.

An ungodly man digs up evil,
and it is on his lips like a burning fire.
Proverbs 16:27

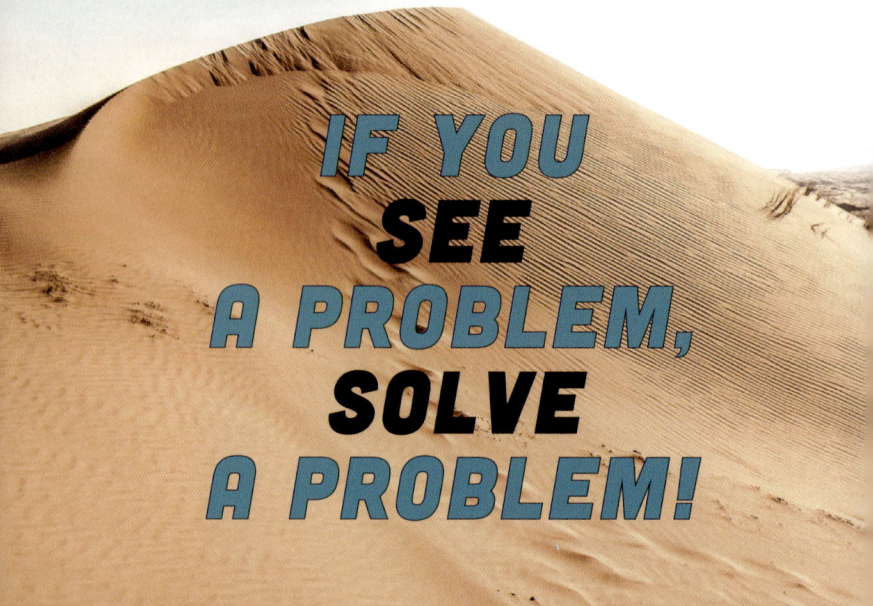

IF YOU
SEE
A PROBLEM,
SOLVE
A PROBLEM!

The silver-haired head is a crown of glory
if it is found in the way of righteousness.

Proverbs 16:31

SOMETIMES AGE AND WISDOM
COME TOGETHER.
SOMETIMES AGE COMES
ALL BY ITSELF!

He who is slow to anger
is better than the mighty,
and he who rules his spirit
than he who takes a city.

Proverbs 16:32

ANGER INTERNALIZED
WILL PRODUCE WRATH THAT IS
VERBALIZED

Better is a dry morsel with quietness
than a house full of feasting with strife.
Proverbs 17:1

UNITY IS NOT
SOUNDING THE SAME.
UNITY IS
SOUNDING TOGETHER.

Better is a dry morsel with quietness
than a house full of feasting with strife.
Proverbs 17:1

BETTER TO DO LESS WITH PEACE THAN MORE WITH STRESS

An evildoer gives heed to false lips.
A liar listens eagerly to a spiteful tongue.

Proverbs 17:4

WHAT YOU PERMIT, YOU PROMOTE.

He who covers a transgression seeks love,
but he who repeats a matter separates friends.

Proverbs 17:9

Blowing out another man's candle will not make yours shine any brighter.

A friend loves at all times,
and a brother is born for adversity.
Proverbs 17:17

LOYALTY
IS REVEALED IN
ADVERSITY

A friend loves at all times,
and a brother is born for adversity.

Proverbs 17:17

THE MOST IMPORTANT
RELATIONSHIPS IN YOUR LIFE
ARE BUILT ON SMALL,
CONSISTENT
DEPOSITS OF TIME.
CONSISTENT,
NOT RANDOM
AVAILABILITY.

A friend loves at all times,
and a brother is born for adversity.

Proverbs 17:17

MANY TIMES, WE ARE WILLING TO
LOVE OTHERS UNCONDITIONALLY...
AS LONG AS THEY
MEET OUR CONDITIONS!

He who has a deceitful heart finds no good,
and he who has a perverse tongue
falls into evil.
Proverbs 17:20

*If you have
Limburger cheese
on your mustache,
all of life will stink.*

He who has a deceitful heart finds no good,
and he who has a perverse tongue
falls into evil.

Proverbs 17:20

IF YOU MEET A JERK
IN THE MORNING,
YOU'VE SIMPLY MET A JERK.
IF YOU MEET JERKS
ALL DAY LONG,
YOU'RE THE JERK!

A merry heart does good like medicine,
but a broken spirit dries the bones.
Proverbs 17:22

*At times, a sense of humor
can be the shortest distance
between any two people.*

A merry heart does good like medicine,
but a broken spirit dries the bones.
Proverbs 17:22

IT'S EASY TO LAUGH
WHEN EVERYTHING IS GOING RIGHT.
IT'S IMPORTANT TO LAUGH
WHEN EVERYTHING IS GOING WRONG.

A man who isolates himself
seeks his own desire.
He rages against all wise judgment.

Proverbs 18:1

YOU MUST HAVE PURPOSE BEYOND YOUR PAIN

A man who isolates himself
seeks his own desire.
He rages against all wise judgment.

Proverbs 18:1

**RELIGION ISOLATES.
RELATIONSHIP INSULATES.
RELIGION REACHES IN.
RELATIONSHIP REACHES OUT.**

A man who isolates himself
seeks his own desire.
He rages against all wise judgment.

Proverbs 18:1

WHEN YOU ARE ALL
WRAPPED UP IN YOURSELF,
IT MAKES FOR A
VERY SMALL PACKAGE.

A fool's mouth is his destruction,
and his lips are the snare of his soul.

Proverbs 18:7

YOU CAN'T HAVE A BAD MOUTH AND A GOOD MARRIAGE.

A man's gift makes room for him
and brings him before great men.
Proverbs 18:16

**Your gift will bring
you into great rooms,
but your character
will keep you there.**

A man's gift makes room for him
and brings him before great men.
Proverbs 18:16

When it comes to your character,
develop your weaknesses.
When it comes to your gifts,
develop your strengths.

A brother offended
is harder to win than a strong city,
and contentions are like the bars of a castle.

Proverbs 18:19

BETRAYAL IS WHAT SOMEONE DOES TO YOU. BITTERNESS IS WHAT YOU DO TO YOURSELF.

JULY

24

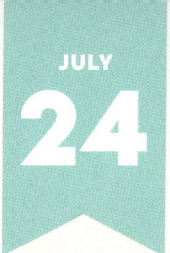

A man's stomach shall be satisfied
from the fruit of his mouth.
From the produce of his lips he shall be filled.

Proverbs 18:20

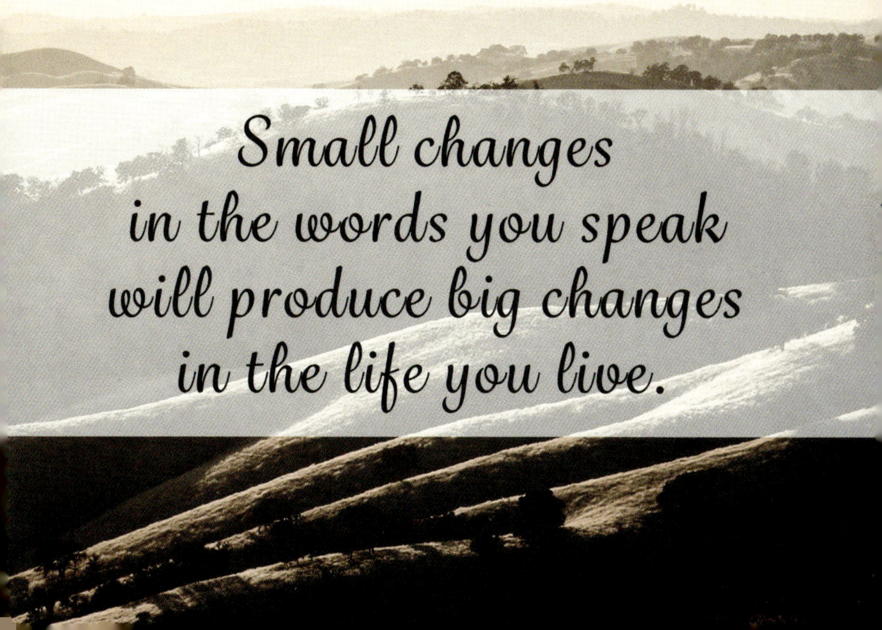

*Small changes
in the words you speak
will produce big changes
in the life you live.*

JULY

25

Death and life are in
the power of the tongue,
and those who love it will eat its fruit.

Proverbs 18:21

DON'T USE YOUR WORDS TO DESCRIBE YOUR LIFE. USE YOUR WORDS TO DESIGN YOUR LIFE.

JULY
26

Death and life are in
the power of the tongue,
and those who love it will eat its fruit.
Proverbs 18:21

GOD CREATED THE WORLD HE WANTED TO LIVE IN

WITH HIS WORDS.
YOU CAN TOO!

A man who has friends
must himself be friendly,
but there is a friend
who sticks closer than a brother.
Proverbs 18:24

**If you try to find a friend,
you won't find them anywhere.
If try to be a friend,
you'll find them everywhere.**

JULY

28

A man who has friends
must himself be friendly,
but there is a friend
who sticks closer than a brother.

Proverbs 18:24

PEOPLE NEED YOU
TO GET CLOSER TO JESUS.
JESUS NEEDS YOU
TO GET CLOSER TO PEOPLE.

It is not good for a soul
to be without knowledge,
and he sins who hastens with his feet.

Proverbs 19:2

IT'S BETTER TO GO TOO SLOW THAN TOO FAST. IT'S EASIER TO PLAY CATCH-UP THAN CLEAN-UP.

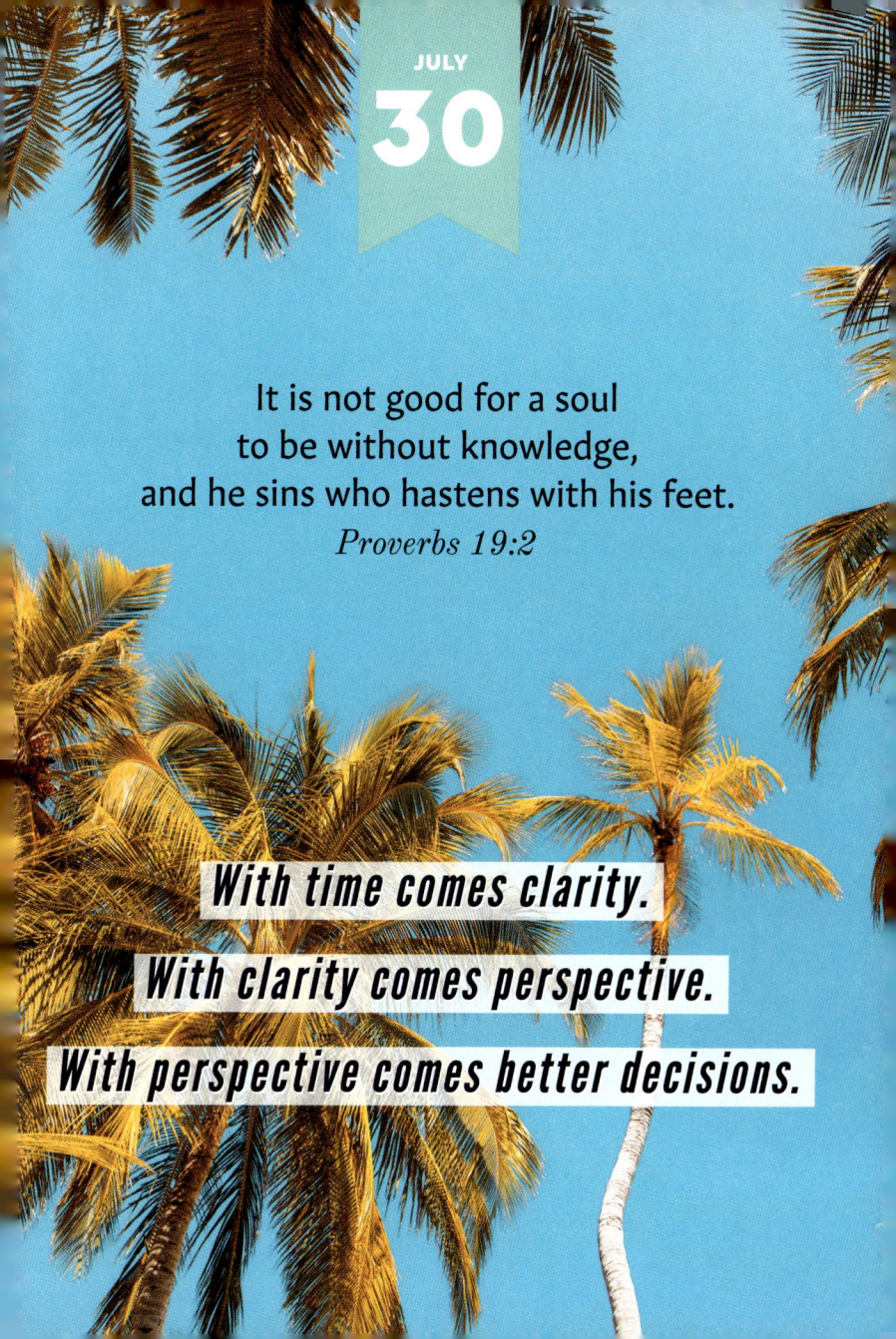

It is not good for a soul
to be without knowledge,
and he sins who hastens with his feet.

Proverbs 19:2

With time comes clarity.

With clarity comes perspective.

With perspective comes better decisions.

It is not good for a soul
to be without knowledge,
and he sins who hastens with his feet.

Proverbs 19:2

BAD INFORMATION
RESULTS IN
A BAD DECISION.
GOOD INFORMATION YIELDS
A GOOD DECISION.
IF THERE IS NO INFORMATION,
AT BEST, THERE WILL BE
NO DECISION.

AUGUST

1

The foolishness of a man twists his way,
and his heart frets against the LORD.
Proverbs 19:3

WE HAVE A GOOD GOD,
BUT WE LIVE IN A CURSED WORLD
WITH A BAD DEVIL
AND STUPID PEOPLE.

The discretion of a man
makes him slow to anger,
and his glory is to overlook a transgression.

Proverbs 19:11

BIG PURPOSE WILL ALWAYS HELP YOU OVERCOME THE CRITICISM OF SMALL PEOPLE

Houses and riches are an
inheritance from fathers,
but a prudent wife is from the LORD.
Proverbs 19:14

THE SECOND MOST IMPORTANT DECISION
YOU WILL EVER MAKE
IS WHO YOU WILL MARRY.

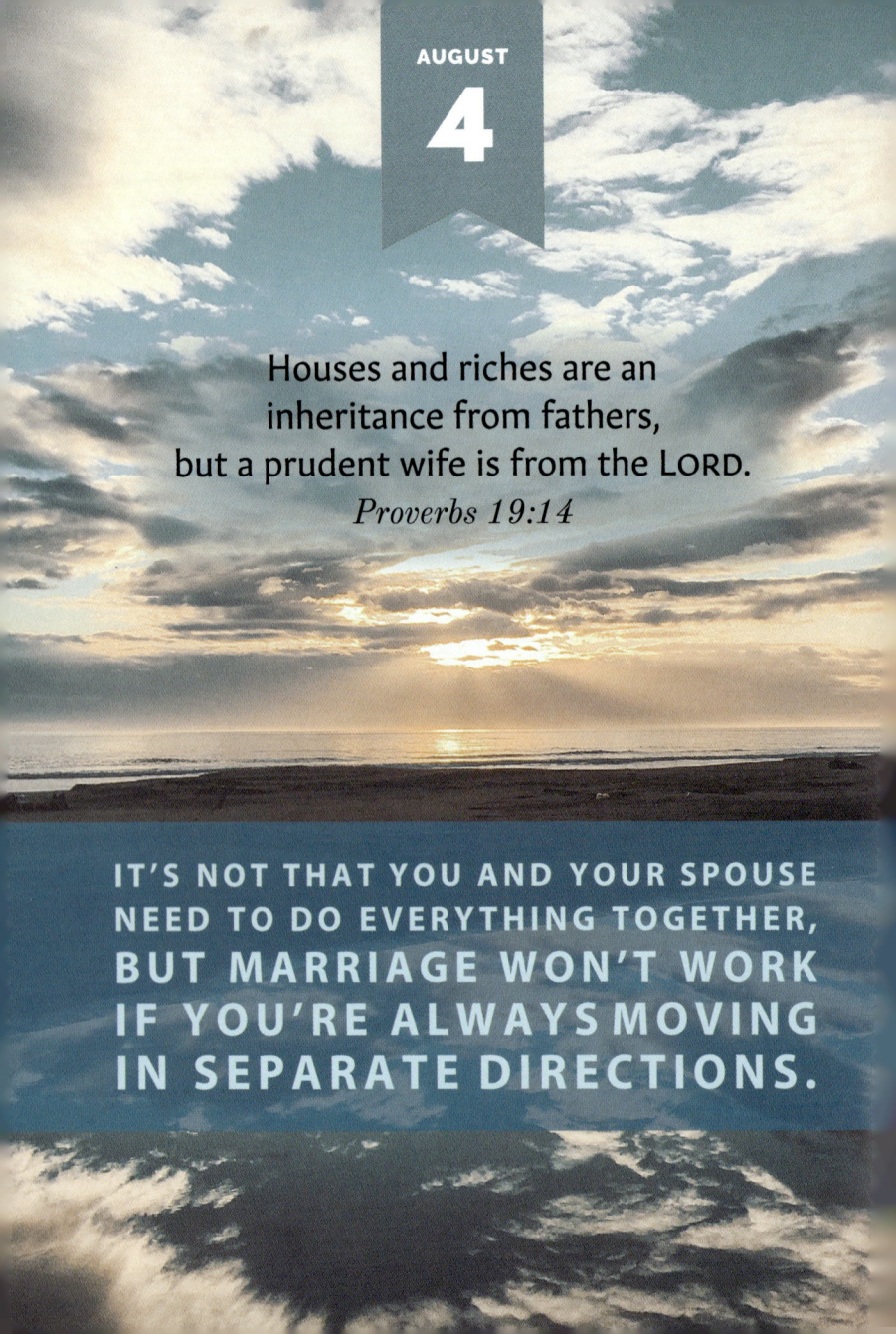

Houses and riches are an
inheritance from fathers,
but a prudent wife is from the LORD.
Proverbs 19:14

IT'S NOT THAT YOU AND YOUR SPOUSE
NEED TO DO EVERYTHING TOGETHER,
BUT MARRIAGE WON'T WORK
IF YOU'RE ALWAYS MOVING
IN SEPARATE DIRECTIONS.

Laziness casts one into a deep sleep,
and an idle person will suffer hunger.
Proverbs 19:15

IF YOU DO THE THINGS YOU NEED TO DO WHEN YOU NEED TO DO THEM, THEN ONE DAY YOU CAN DO THE THINGS YOU WANT TO DO WHEN YOU WANT TO DO THEM.

He who keeps the commandment
keeps his soul, but he who is
careless of his ways will die.

Proverbs 19:16

TRYING
IS FILLED
WITH
GOOD
INTENTIONS

DOING
IS FILLED
WITH
INTENTIONAL
GOOD

Chasten your son while there is hope,
and do not set your heart
on his destruction.

Proverbs 19:18

YOUR CHILD
NEEDS A PARENT,
NOT A FRIEND.
BUT IF YOU
PARENT HIM
IN THE BEGINNING,
YOU'LL HAVE A FRIEND
IN THE END.

A man of great wrath will suffer punishment.
For if you rescue him,
you will have to do it again.

Proverbs 19:19

CONSEQUENCES ARE A TEACHER. REMOVING A MAN FROM HIS CONSEQUENCES ONLY PERPETUATES HIS ACTIONS.

AUGUST

9

Listen to counsel and receive instruction,
that you may be wise in your latter days.

Proverbs 19:20

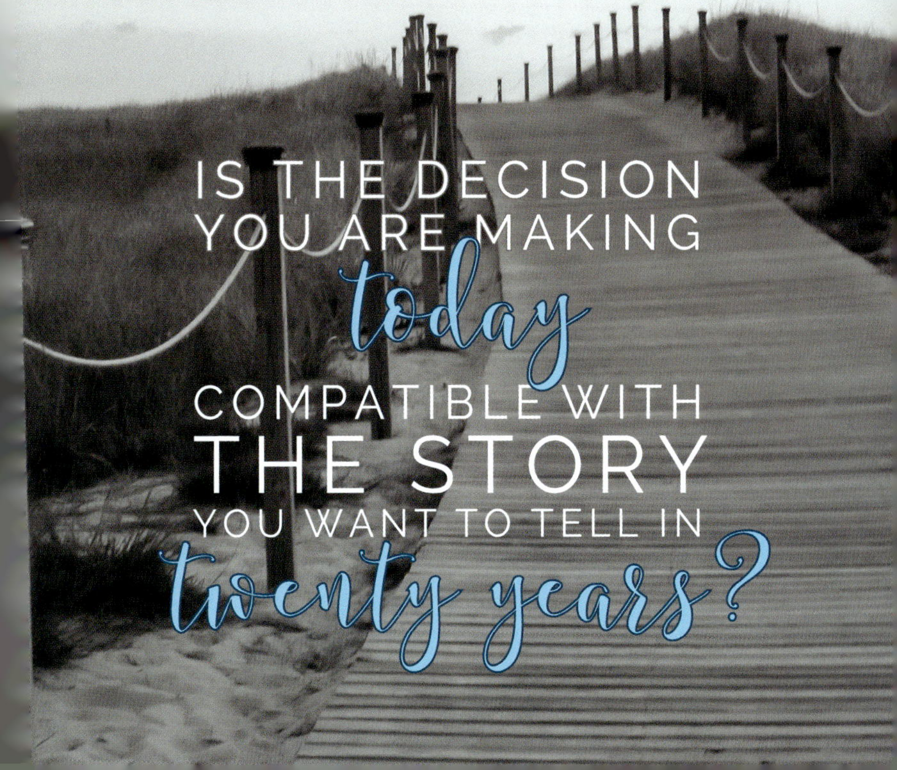

IS THE DECISION
YOU ARE MAKING
today
COMPATIBLE WITH
THE STORY
YOU WANT TO TELL IN
twenty years?

Listen to counsel and receive instruction,
that you may be wise in your latter days.

Proverbs 19:20

INVEST IN KNOWLEDGE NOW, AND IT WILL COMPOUND IN WISDOM LATER.

What is desired in a man is kindness.

Proverbs 19:22a

Sympathy
MOVES YOU TO TEARS.

Compassion
MOVES YOU TO ACTION.

What is desired in a man is kindness.
Proverbs 19:22a

FEELINGS
ARE NOT
ALWAYS RIGHT,
BUT THEY
ARE ALWAYS
REAL

What is desired in a man is kindness.
Proverbs 19:22a

IT'S EASY TO UNDERESTIMATE THE POWER OF A TINY TOUCH OF KINDNESS

Cease listening to instruction, my son,
and you will stray from the words of knowledge.

Proverbs 19:27

COMMITMENT
MEANS STAYING LOYAL TO
WHAT YOU SAID YOU WOULD DO
LONG AFTER THE MOOD YOU SAID IT IN
HAS LEFT YOU

AUGUST
15

Wine is a mocker,
strong drink is a brawler,
and whoever is led astray by it is not wise.
Proverbs 20:1

Addiction occurs when you no longer have it but it has you

Most men will proclaim
each his own goodness,
but who can find a faithful man?

Proverbs 20:6

IF YOU'RE TOO BIG TO DO LITTLE THINGS, THEN YOU'RE TOO LITTLE TO DO BIG THINGS.

Most men will proclaim
each his own goodness,
but who can find a faithful man?
Proverbs 20:6

YOUR DAILY DECISIONS MUST MATCH THE SIZE OF YOUR VISION.

The righteous man walks in his integrity.

Proverbs 20:7a

GOD WILL INITIALLY PLACE YOU IN AN ASSIGNMENT SMALLER THAN YOUR GIFT. THIS IS BECAUSE YOUR CHARACTER IS ALWAYS MORE IMPORTANT THAN YOUR GIFT.

The righteous man walks in his integrity.

Proverbs 20:7a

CHARISMA LIKES EASY BUT QUITS AT HARD. *CHARACTER* LIKES EASY BUT QUITS AT NOTHING!

The righteous man walks in his integrity.
Proverbs 20:7a

PERSONALITY IS
WHO YOU ARE IN PUBLIC.
CHARACTER IS
WHO YOU ARE IN PRIVATE.

AUGUST

21

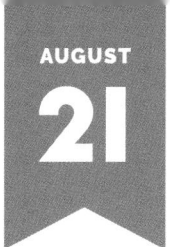

The righteous man walks in his integrity.
His children are blessed after him.

Proverbs 20:7

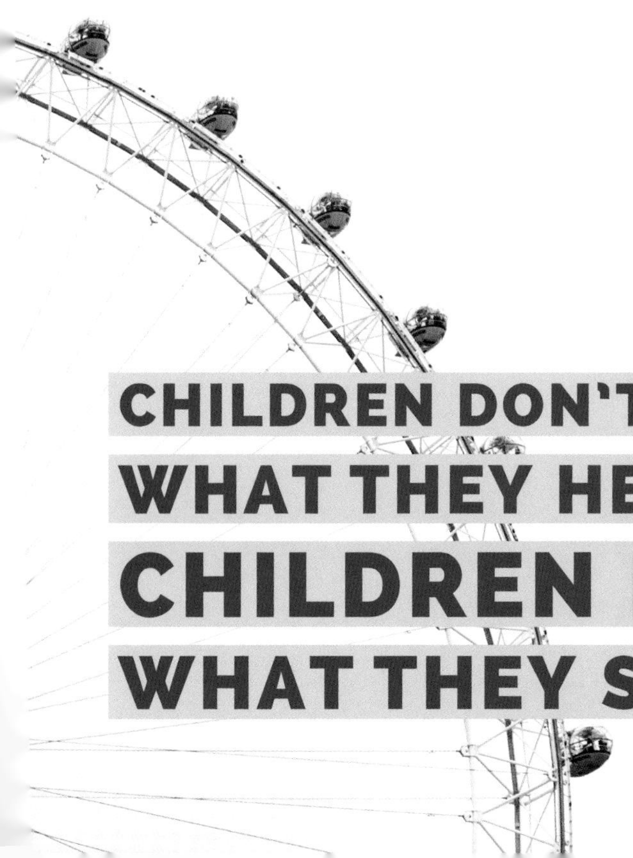

CHILDREN DON'T DO WHAT THEY HEAR. CHILDREN DO WHAT THEY SEE.

The righteous man walks in his integrity.
His children are blessed after him.

Proverbs 20:7

Character is
not just taught
to your children.
Character is
caught by
your children.

The righteous man walks in his integrity.
His children are blessed after him.

Proverbs 20:7a

IF YOU WANT YOUR CHILD TO BELIEVE GOD'S WORD, THEY MUST SEE YOU KEEPING YOUR WORD.

An inheritance gained hastily
at the beginning
will not be blessed at the end.
Proverbs 20:21

YOU WILL EVENTUALLY LOSE ANYTHING YOU COMPROMISE TO GAIN.

It is a snare for a man
to devote rashly something as holy
and afterward to reconsider his vows.

Proverbs 20:25

Time is your friend.

Learn to wait.

Many times, you can't see now

what you will see later.

Mercy and truth preserve the king,
and by lovingkindness
he upholds his throne.

Proverbs 20:28

TRUTH WITHOUT GRACE
IS MEAN.
GRACE WITHOUT TRUTH
IS MEANINGLESS.

The plans of the diligent lead surely to plenty,
but those of everyone who is hasty,
surely to poverty.

Proverbs 21:5

DILIGENCE IS DOING LITTLE THINGS FOR A LONG TIME UNTIL IT MAKES A BIG DIFFERENCE.

The plans of the diligent lead surely to plenty, but those of everyone who is hasty, surely to poverty.

Proverbs 21:5

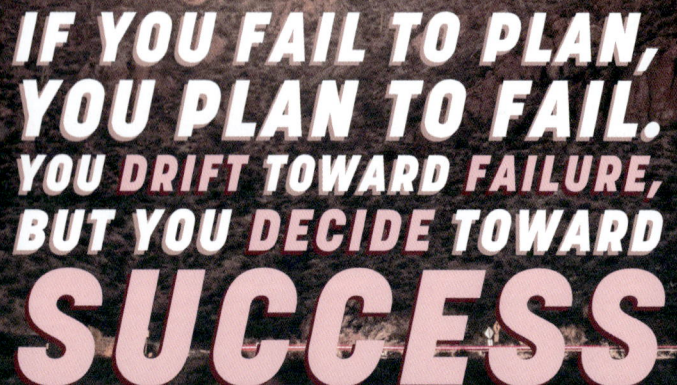

IF YOU FAIL TO PLAN, YOU PLAN TO FAIL. YOU DRIFT TOWARD FAILURE, BUT YOU DECIDE TOWARD SUCCESS

AUGUST

29

The plans of the diligent lead surely to plenty,
but those of everyone who is hasty,
surely to poverty.

Proverbs 21:5

WORRY
FACES THE FUTURE
WITH FEAR.
PLANNING
FACES THE
FUTURE
WITH FAITH.

Whoever guards his mouth and tongue
keeps his soul from troubles.

Proverbs 21:23

**YOUR LIFE CONSISTS OF
THE DECISIONS YOU MAKE,
THE ACTIONS YOU TAKE,
AND THE WORDS YOU SPEAK.**

The desire of the lazy man kills him,
for his hands refuse to labor.

Proverbs 21:25

DON'T JUST DESIRE RESULTS.

REQUIRE THEM!

The horse is prepared for the day of battle,
but deliverance is of the LORD.

Proverbs 21:31

OBEDIENCE IS YOUR RESPONSIBILITY.

OUTCOME IS GOD'S

SEPTEMBER

2

The horse is prepared for the day of battle,
but deliverance is of the LORD.

Proverbs 21:31

IN LIFE,
YOU WILL
EITHER BE
PREPARING OR
REPAIRING

The horse is prepared for the day of battle,
but deliverance is of the LORD.

Proverbs 21:31

EXPECTATION

b r e e d s

PREPARATION

SEPTEMBER

4

A good name is to be chosen
rather than great riches,
loving favor rather than silver and gold.
Proverbs 22:1

YOU CHOOSE THE QUALITY
OF YOUR NAME
BY THE QUALITY
OF YOUR CHOICES

A good name is to be chosen
rather than great riches,
loving favor rather than silver and gold.

Proverbs 22:1

YOU ARE NOT A LOSER. YOU ARE A CHOOSER!

A good name is to be chosen
rather than great riches,
loving favor rather than silver and gold.

Proverbs 22:1

FINISH STRONG. YOUR LAST IMPRESSION WILL BE YOUR LASTING IMPRESSION.

7

A good name is to be chosen
rather than great riches,
loving favor rather than silver and gold.

Proverbs 22:1

HOW YOU LIVE
YOUR LIFE TODAY
WILL DETERMINE
WHAT OTHERS SAY ABOUT YOU
AT YOUR FUNERAL

By humility and the fear of the LORD
are riches and honor and life.

Proverbs 22:4

UNSUCCESSFUL PEOPLE
SPEND THEIR LIFE
WITH TIME.
SUCCESSFUL PEOPLE
SPEND THEIR TIME
WITH LIFE.

By humility and the fear of the LORD
are riches and honor and life.

Proverbs 22:4

IT'S HIS GOODNESS
THAT CAUSES US
TO APPROACH HIM

IT'S HIS GREATNESS
THAT CAUSES US
TO REVERE HIM

By humility and the fear of the LORD
are riches and honor and life.

Proverbs 22:4

SOME PEOPLE
ARE AFRAID TO DIE

OTHERS ARE AFRAID TO

LIVE

Train up a child in the way he should go,
and when he is old he will not depart from it.

Proverbs 22:6

WHEN CHILDREN ARE YOUNG,
YOU SHOULD TEACH THEM.

WHEN CHILDREN ARE TEENS,
YOU SHOULD TRAIN THEM.

WHEN CHILDREN ARE ADULTS,
YOU SHOULD TRUST THEM.

Train up a child in the way he should go,
and when he is old he will not depart from it.
Proverbs 22:6

YOUR CHILD'S DESIGN REVEALS THEIR DESTINY

Train up a child in the way he should go,
and when he is old he will not depart from it.

Proverbs 22:6

CHILDREN
DON'T NEED A
COOL PARENT.
THEY NEED A
CONSISTENT PARENT.

Train up a child in the way he should go,
and when he is old he will not depart from it.

Proverbs 22:6

AFFECTION WITHOUT ATTENTION AND AUTHORITY MEANS YOU ARE TRYING TO BE THE CHILD'S FRIEND AND NOT THEIR PARENT

He who has a generous eye will be blessed,
for he gives of his bread to the poor.

Proverbs 22:9

You can't be a
SELFISH
PERSON
and lead a
SIGNIFICANT
LIFE

He who has a generous eye will be blessed,
for he gives of his bread to the poor.

Proverbs 22:9

WITH ONE MINOR EXCEPTION, THE WORLD'S ENTIRE POPULATION CONSISTS OF SOMEONE OTHER THAN YOU!

He who has a generous eye will be blessed,
for he gives of his bread to the poor.

Proverbs 22:9

A RICH PERSON
WHO IS STINGY
IS SIMPLY
A POOR PERSON
WITH MONEY

SEPTEMBER

18

Cast out the scoffer, and contention will leave.
Yes, strife and reproach will cease.
Proverbs 22:10

NEVER DISCUSS YOUR FUTURE WITH THOSE WHO DO NOT SEE THEMSELVES IN IT.

Foolishness is bound up in the heart of a child.
The rod of correction will drive it far from him.
Proverbs 22:15

FUN LIFTS PEOPLE. FOOLISHNESS HURTS PEOPLE.

Do not remove the ancient landmark
which your fathers have set.

Proverbs 22:28

YOU CAN'T BE
THANKFUL AND ENTITLED
AT THE SAME TIME

THE MAN WHO
DRINKS THE WATER
MUST REMEMBER
THE MAN WHO
DUG THE WELL

Do you see a man who excels in his work?
He will stand before kings.
He will not stand before unknown men.

Proverbs 22:29

EXCELLENCE WILL ALWAYS GET YOU NOTICED

Do you see a man who excels in his work?
He will stand before kings.
He will not stand before unknown men.
Proverbs 22:29

NO ONE STANDS IN LINE FOR AVERAGE

Do you see a man who excels in his work?
He will stand before kings.
He will not stand before unknown men.
Proverbs 22:29

AVERAGE

IS THE TOP OF THE BOTTOM, THE BOTTOM OF THE TOP, THE BEST OF THE WORST, AND THE WORST OF THE BEST!

Do not overwork to be rich.
Because of your own understanding, cease!

Proverbs 23:4

GOOD LEADERS
DON'T DO MORE.
THEY DO MORE OF
WHAT MATTERS
MOST

SEPTEMBER

25

Do not overwork to be rich.
Because of your own understanding, cease!

Proverbs 23:4

AN OVERWHELMED SCHEDULE
WILL PRODUCE
AN UNDERWHELMED SOUL

Will you set your eyes on that which is not?
For riches certainly make themselves wings.
They fly away like an eagle toward heaven.
Proverbs 23:5

THE DEVIL'S BIGGEST LIE
HAS ALWAYS BEEN
"THE ONE THING
YOU DON'T HAVE
IS THE ONE THING
YOU NEED TO BE HAPPY."

For as he thinks in his heart, so is he.

Proverbs 23:7a

IF YOU THINK THE WAY YOU USED TO THINK, YOU'LL DO THE THINGS YOU USED TO DO.

SEPTEMBER

28

For as he thinks in his heart, so is he.

Proverbs 23:7a

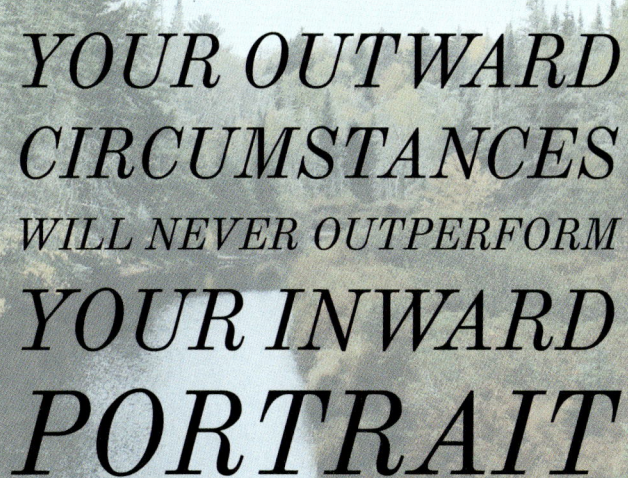

YOUR OUTWARD CIRCUMSTANCES WILL NEVER OUTPERFORM YOUR INWARD PORTRAIT

For as he thinks in his heart, so is he.

Proverbs 23:7a

YOUR LIFE WILL ALWAYS MOVE IN THE DIRECTION OF YOUR PREDOMINANT THOUGHTS

SEPTEMBER

30

For as he thinks in his heart, so is he.
Proverbs 23:7a

YOU DON'T SEE LIFE

AS IT IS

YOU SEE LIFE

AS YOU ARE

Apply your heart to instruction,
and your ears to words of knowledge.
Proverbs 23:12

TRUE POWER
IS THE KNOWLEDGE OF WHAT TO DO
IN ANY SITUATION
TO BRING VICTORY

OCTOBER

2

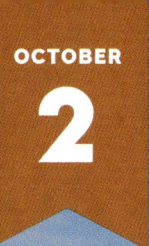

For surely there is a hereafter,
and your hope will not be cut off.
Proverbs 23:18

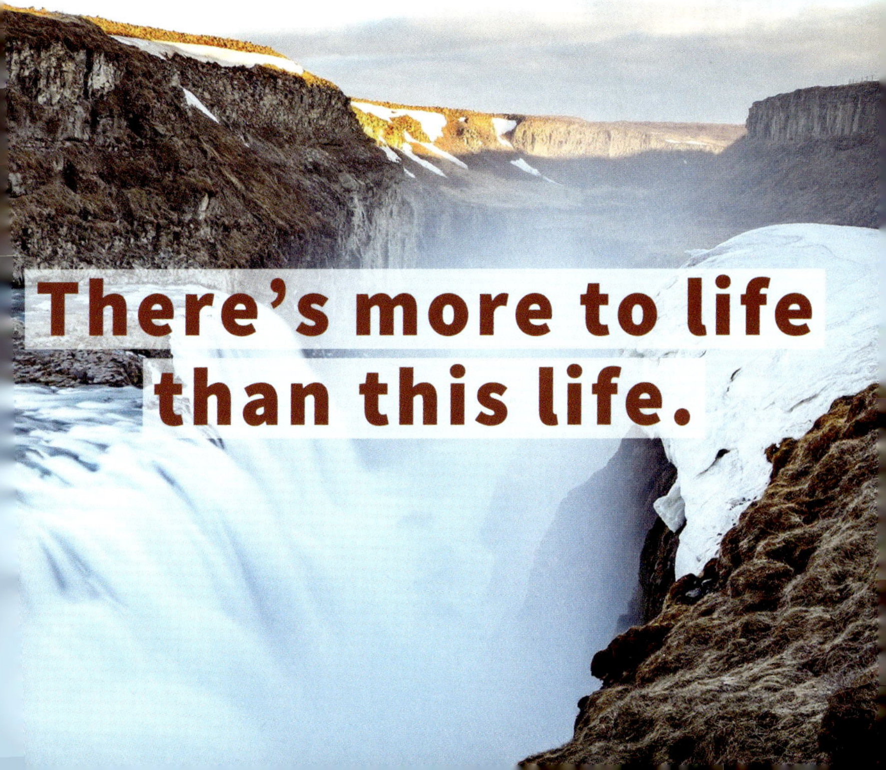

There's more to life than this life.

For surely there is a hereafter,
and your hope will not be cut off.
Proverbs 23:18

NEVER LOWER YOUR EXPECTATIONS FOR EARTH. SIMPLY RAISE YOUR EXPECTATIONS FOR HEAVEN.

OCTOBER

4

For surely there is a hereafter,
and your hope will not be cut off.
Proverbs 23:18

DETERMINE
THAT YOU
DON'T WANT
EARTHLY
REWARDS
MORE THAN
ETERNAL
ACCOLADES

Do not be envious of evil men,
nor desire to be with them.
For their heart devises violence,
and their lips talk of troublemaking.

Proverbs 24:1-2

IF YOU ARE ALWAYS GETTING KICKED IN THE REAR, CHANCES ARE YOU ARE OUT FRONT LEADING!

If you faint in the day of adversity,
your strength is small.

Proverbs 24:10

CHAMPIONS ARE NOT PEOPLE WHO DON'T FAIL

CHAMPIONS ARE PEOPLE WHO DON'T QUIT

If you faint in the day of adversity,
your strength is small.

Proverbs 24:10

COURAGE IS SIMPLY DOING IT AFRAID.

If you faint in the day of adversity,
your strength is small.
Proverbs 24:10

FAILING
IS AN ACT.
FAILURE IS AN
ATTITUDE.
GET UP!

Deliver those who are drawn toward death,
and hold back those stumbling to the slaughter.

Proverbs 24:11

QUIT TELLING PEOPLE WHAT'S
WRONG WITH THEM,
AND START TELLING
THEM WHAT HAPPENED TO YOU.

Deliver those who are drawn toward death,
and hold back those stumbling to the slaughter.
Proverbs 24:11

CONNECT
BEFORE YOU
CORRECT

For a righteous man may fall
seven times and rise again,
but the wicked shall fall by calamity.
Proverbs 24:16

**FAILURE IS SIMPLY THE
OPPORTUNITY
TO BEGIN AGAIN
MORE INTELLIGENTLY**

For a righteous man may fall
seven times and rise again,
but the wicked shall fall by calamity.

Proverbs 24:16

YOU CAN NEVER QUIT YOUR WAY TO SUCCESS

For a righteous man may fall
seven times and rise again,
but the wicked shall fall by calamity.

Proverbs 24:16

VICTORY IS SIMPLY GETTING UP
ONE MORE TIME
THAN YOU'VE FALLEN

OCTOBER

14

My son, fear the LORD and the king.
Do not associate with those given to change.
Proverbs 24:21

ASSOCIATION GIVES YOU
MOTIVATION FOR YOUR
DESTINATION

OCTOBER
15

My son, fear the LORD and the king.
Do not associate with those given to change.
Proverbs 24:21

IF YOU WANT TO MAKE
WISE DECISIONS,
ASSOCIATE YOURSELF
WITH WISER PEOPLE.

My son, fear the LORD and the king.
Do not associate with those given to change.
Proverbs 24:21

YOU WILL ALWAYS
RISE OR COMPROMISE
TO THE LEVEL OF YOUR
ASSOCIATION

I went by the field of the lazy man and by the
vineyard of the man devoid of understanding,
and there it was, all overgrown with thorns.
Its surface was covered with nettles.
Its stone wall was broken down.
When I saw it, I considered it well.
I looked on it and received instruction.

Proverbs 24:30-32

ANOTHER MAN'S PAIN
SHOULD BE YOUR
WISDOM

OCTOBER

18

I went by the field of the lazy man and by the vineyard of the man devoid of understanding, and there it was, all overgrown with thorns. Its surface was covered with nettles. Its stone wall was broken down. When I saw it, I considered it well. I looked on it and received instruction. A little sleep, a little slumber, a little folding of the hands to rest. So shall your poverty come like a prowler and your need like an armed man.

Proverbs 24:30-34

LAZINESS IS NEGLECTING LITTLE THINGS FOR A LONG TIME UNTIL IT MAKES A BIG DIFFERENCE

Do not go hastily to court,
for what will you do in the end
when your neighbor has put you to shame?
Debate your case with your neighbor,
and do not disclose the secret to another.

Proverbs 25:8-9

IT'S NOT ABOUT WHO IS RIGHT
BUT MAKING THINGS RIGHT.

RESOLUTION
IS THE SOLUTION

Do not go hastily to court,
for what will you do in the end
when your neighbor has put you to shame?
Debate your case with your neighbor,
and do not disclose the secret to another.
Proverbs 25:8-9

YOU DON'T TRULY KNOW SOMEONE UNTIL YOU DISAGREE WITH THEM.

A word fitly spoken is like apples of gold
in settings of silver.

Proverbs 25:11

HOW DO YOU IDENTIFY SOMEONE WHO NEEDS ENCOURAGEMENT? IF THEY'RE BREATHING!

Like the cold of snow in time of harvest
is a faithful messenger to those who send him,
for he refreshes the soul of his masters.

Proverbs 25:13

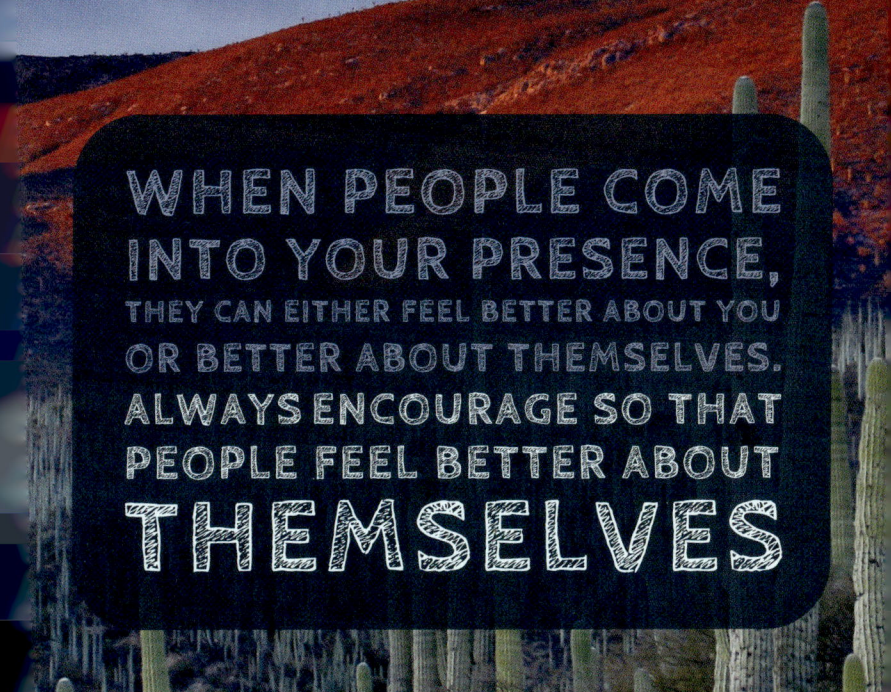

WHEN PEOPLE COME
INTO YOUR PRESENCE,
THEY CAN EITHER FEEL BETTER ABOUT YOU
OR BETTER ABOUT THEMSELVES.
ALWAYS ENCOURAGE SO THAT
PEOPLE FEEL BETTER ABOUT
THEMSELVES

OCTOBER

23

Confidence in an unfaithful man
in time of trouble is like a bad tooth
and a foot out of joint.

Proverbs 25:19

YOUR UNFAITHFULNESS TODAY

DISQUALIFIES YOU

FROM A BETTER TOMORROW.

OCTOBER

24

Confidence in an unfaithful man
in time of trouble is like a bad tooth
and a foot out of joint.

Proverbs 25:19

IF YOU CAN'T TRUST A PERSON
AT ALL POINTS,
YOU CAN'T TRUST THAT PERSON
AT ANY POINT.

Confidence in an unfaithful man
in time of trouble is like a bad tooth
and a foot out of joint.

Proverbs 25:19

TRUST
IN INCREMENTS

If your enemy is hungry, give him bread to eat.
And if he is thirsty, give him water to drink.
For so you will heap coals of fire on his head,
and the LORD will reward you.

Proverbs 25:21-22

FORGIVENESS
IS THE ABILITY TO LET GO
OF YOUR DESIRE FOR
VENGEANCE
WITHOUT LETTING GO
OF YOUR DESIRE FOR
JUSTICE

If your enemy is hungry, give him bread to eat.
And if he is thirsty, give him water to drink.
For so you will heap coals of fire on his head,
and the LORD will reward you.

Proverbs 25:21-22

CEASE TO
FOCUS ON THE REWARD,
AND YOU WILL CEASE TO
PAY THE COST

A righteous man
who falters before the wicked
is like a murky spring and a polluted well.

Proverbs 25:26

YOUR LIFE SHOULD
ALWAYS
SPEAK LOUDER
THAN YOUR LIPS

A righteous man
who falters before the wicked
is like a murky spring and a polluted well.

Proverbs 25:26

YOU CAN HELP OTHERS FROM A PLACE OF MORAL AUTHORITY. YOU CAN HURT OTHERS FROM A PLACE OF SUPERIORITY OR MORAL HYPOCRISY.

As a dog returns to his own vomit,
so a fool repeats his folly.

Proverbs 26:11

ONLY A FOOL
TRIPS OVER WHAT IS
BEHIND HIM

OCTOBER
31

The lazy man says, "There is a lion in the road!
A fierce lion is in the streets!"
Proverbs 26:13

It's easier to go from
failure to success
than excuse to success

The lazy man says, "There is a lion in the road!
A fierce lion is in the streets!"

Proverbs 26:13

YOU'RE EITHER
MAKING EXCUSES OR
PROGRESS,
BUT NOT BOTH.

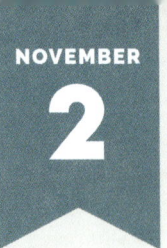

The lazy man says,
"There is a lion in the road!
A fierce lion is in the streets!"
Proverbs 26:13

You can't blame your way into a successful future

The lazy man says,
"There is a lion in the road!
A fierce lion is in the streets!"
Proverbs 26:13

THE MAN WHO EXCUSES HIS WAY OUT CAN ALWAYS FIND A THOUSAND EXITS.

He who passes by and meddles
in a quarrel not his own
is like one who takes a dog by the ears.
Proverbs 26:17

IF YOU PICK UP A BATTLE YOU'RE NOT
ANOINTED TO FIGHT,
YOU'LL PICK UP A BURDEN YOU'RE NOT
ANOINTED TO BEAR.

He who passes by and meddles
in a quarrel not his own
is like one who takes a dog by the ears.

Proverbs 26:17

IN LIFE, IT'S IMPORTANT
TO DISCERN WHICH FIRE
HAS THE POTENTIAL TO BLAZE
AND WHICH FIRE WILL SIMPLY
SMOLDER AND BURN OUT.
YOU CAN'T SPEND YOUR LIFE
PUTTING OUT FIRES!

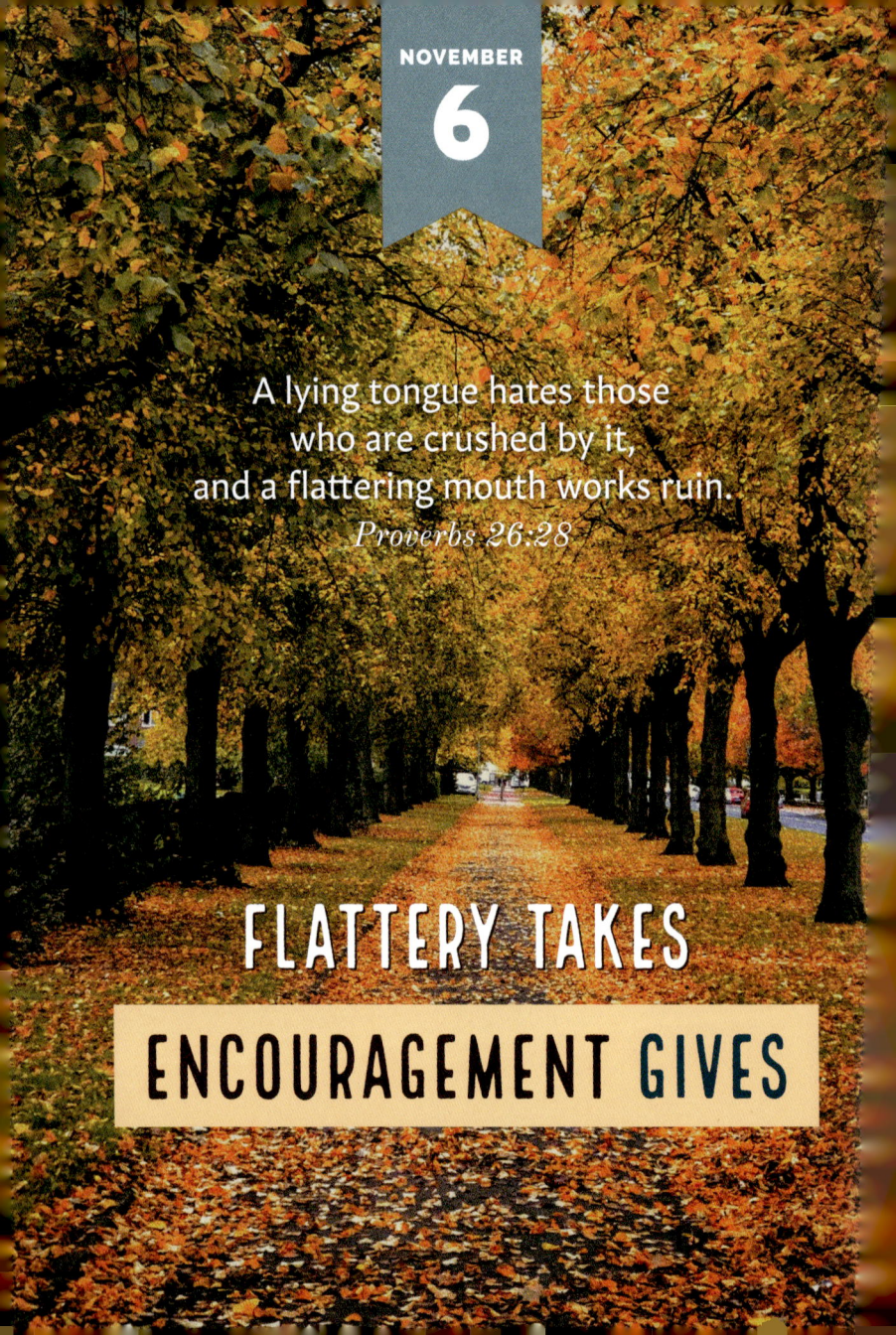

A lying tongue hates those
who are crushed by it,
and a flattering mouth works ruin.
Proverbs 26:28

FLATTERY TAKES

ENCOURAGEMENT GIVES

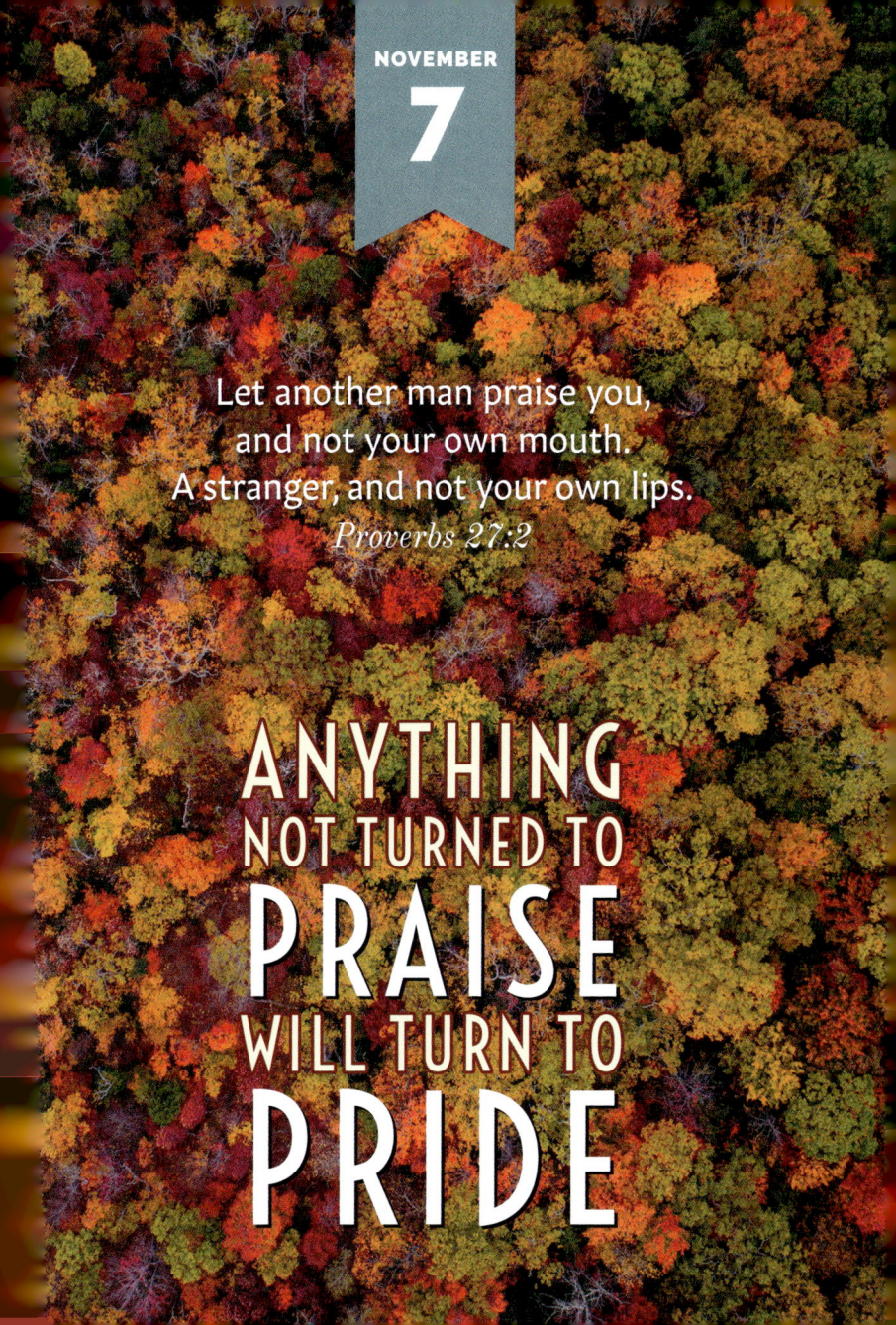

NOVEMBER

7

Let another man praise you,
and not your own mouth.
A stranger, and not your own lips.
Proverbs 27:2

ANYTHING
NOT TURNED TO
PRAISE
WILL TURN TO
PRIDE

Faithful are the wounds of a friend,
but the kisses of an enemy
are deceitful.

Proverbs 27:6

Love quickly, but trust slowly.

Faithful are the wounds of a friend,
but the kisses of an enemy
are deceitful.

Proverbs 27:6

YOUR VULNERABLE RELATIONSHIPS ARE YOUR VALUABLE RELATIONSHIPS

NOVEMBER
10

A satisfied soul loathes the honeycomb,
but to a hungry soul
every bitter thing is sweet.

Proverbs 27:7

DON'T GET BITTER.
Get better!

Like a bird that wanders from its nest
is a man who wanders from his place.
Proverbs 27:8

DON'T RUN IN TOUGH TIMES.
THE PROCESS THAT WILL TAKE YOU
WHERE YOU NEED TO GO
MUST BE LEARNED
RIGHT WHERE YOU ARE

Ointment and perfume delight the heart,
and the sweetness of a man's friend
gives delight by hearty counsel.

Proverbs 27:9

YOUR THREE CLOSEST FRIENDS ARE A REFLECTION OF YOU. YOUR THREE CLOSEST FRIENDS ARE A REFLECTION OF YOUR FUTURE.

A prudent man foresees evil
and hides himself.
The simple pass on and are punished.
Proverbs 27:12

DISCRETION IS WISDOM
THAT KEEPS YOU FROM
FUTURE TROUBLE

He who blesses his friend with a loud voice,
rising early in the morning,
it will be counted a curse to him.

Proverbs 27:14

DO THE
RIGHT THING
AT THE RIGHT TIME

NOVEMBER

15

Hell and Destruction are never full.
So the eyes of man are never satisfied.
Proverbs 27:20

DON'T FOCUS ON
WHAT YOU DON'T HAVE.
FOCUS ON
WHAT YOU DO HAVE.

Hell and Destruction are never full.
So the eyes of man are never satisfied.

Proverbs 27:20

DON'T FOCUS ON
HOW FAR YOU NEED TO GO.
FOCUS ON HOW FAR YOU'VE COME.

NOVEMBER

17

The wicked flee when no one pursues,
but the righteous are bold as a lion.

Proverbs 28:1

WHEN YOU STEP OUT IN
BOLDNESS
GOD WILL MEET YOU WITH
HIS POWER

He who covers his sins will not prosper,
but whoever confesses and forsakes them
will have mercy.

Proverbs 28:13

ADMIT IT. QUIT IT.
THEN FORGET IT!

NOVEMBER

19

He who covers his sins will not prosper,
but whoever confesses and forsakes them
will have mercy.

Proverbs 28:13

TELL THE TRUTH.
TELL IT EARLY.
TELL IT YOURSELF.
TELL IT ALL.

He who covers his sins will not prosper,
but whoever confesses and forsakes them
will have mercy.

Proverbs 28:13

GOD IS NOT A REPLACER.

GOD IS A REPAIRER!

He who covers his sins will not prosper,
but whoever confesses and forsakes them
will have mercy.

Proverbs 28:13

WHEN YOU MESS UP,

FESS UP.

DON'T COVER UP!

He who covers his sins will not prosper,
but whoever confesses and forsakes them
will have mercy.

Proverbs 28:13

GUILT, REGRET, AND PITY

WILL ONLY KEEP YOU STUCK IN THE PAST.

He who covers his sins will not prosper,
but whoever confesses and forsakes them
will have mercy.

Proverbs 28:13

IT'S NOT WHAT YOU DO WHEN YOU SIN THAT COUNTS.

IT'S WHAT YOU DO AFTER YOU SIN.

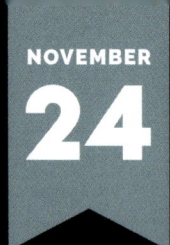

NOVEMBER

24

He who covers his sins will not prosper,
but whoever confesses and forsakes them
will have mercy.

Proverbs 28:13

DON'T RUN FROM GOD. RUN TO GOD.
WHEN YOU CONFESS IT
IS NOT WHEN HE
FOUND OUT ABOUT IT.

Happy is the man who is always reverent,
but he who hardens his heart
will fall into calamity.

Proverbs 28:14

WORSHIP IS NOT JUST THE SONGS YOU SING. WORSHIP IS THE LIFE YOU LIVE.

Happy is the man who is always reverent,
but he who hardens his heart
will fall into calamity.

Proverbs 28:14

GOD WANTS YOU
TENDERHEARTED AND
TOUGH-SKINNED.
THE DEVIL WANTS YOU
HARDHEARTED AND TENDER-SKINNED.

Whoever walks blamelessly will be saved,
but he who is perverse in his ways
will suddenly fall.

Proverbs 28:18

LEAD THROUGH INSPIRATION, NOT INTIMIDATION.

NOVEMBER

28

He who tills his land will have plenty of bread,
but he who follows frivolity
will have poverty enough!

Proverbs 28:19

INCONSISTENCY
PRODUCES
MEDIOCRITY

NOVEMBER

29

He who tills his land will have plenty of bread,
but he who follows frivolity
will have poverty enough!

Proverbs 28:19

THERE IS A BIG DIFFERENCE BETWEEN GOOD INTENTIONS AND LIVING INTENTIONALLY

He who tills his land
will have plenty of bread,
but he who follows frivolity
will have poverty enough!
Proverbs 28:19

THERE IS A GREAT PLACE TO GO
IF YOU ARE BROKE...
TO WORK!

DECEMBER

I

A faithful man will abound with blessings,
but he who hastens to be rich
will not go unpunished.

Proverbs 28:20

IT'S THE
SMALL CHANGES
THAT NO ONE SEES
THAT CREATE THE
BIG THINGS
THAT EVERYONE
WANTS

A faithful man will abound with blessings,
but he who hastens to be rich
will not go unpunished.

Proverbs 28:20

GOD WILL EVALUATE YOU IN THE SMALL TO DETERMINE IF YOU ARE READY FOR BIG

A faithful man will abound with blessings,
but he who hastens to be rich
will not go unpunished.

Proverbs 28:20

If you won't be
faithful in the rehearsal,
you won't be
found in the recital.

A faithful man will abound with blessings,
but he who hastens to be rich
will not go unpunished.

Proverbs 28:20

BIG NEVER SPRINGS FROM NOTHING. BIG ALWAYS SPRINGS FROM LITTLE.

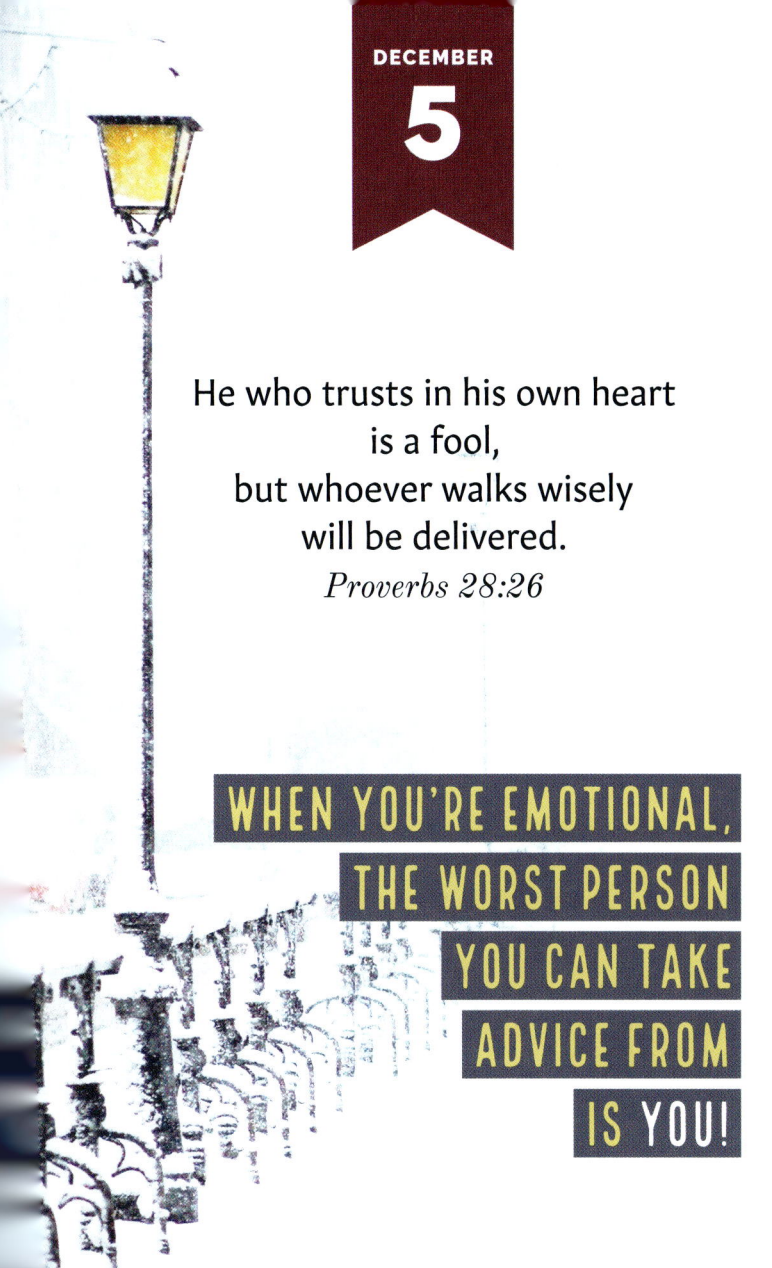

He who trusts in his own heart
is a fool,
but whoever walks wisely
will be delivered.
Proverbs 28:26

WHEN YOU'RE EMOTIONAL,
THE WORST PERSON
YOU CAN TAKE
ADVICE FROM
IS YOU!

A fool vents all his feelings,
but a wise man holds them back.

Proverbs 29:11

WHEN EMOTIONS ARE HIGH, WISDOM IS LOW.

DECEMBER
7

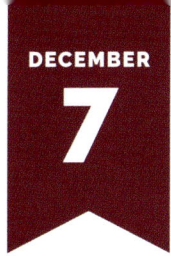

A fool vents all his feelings,
but a wise man holds them back.

Proverbs 29:11

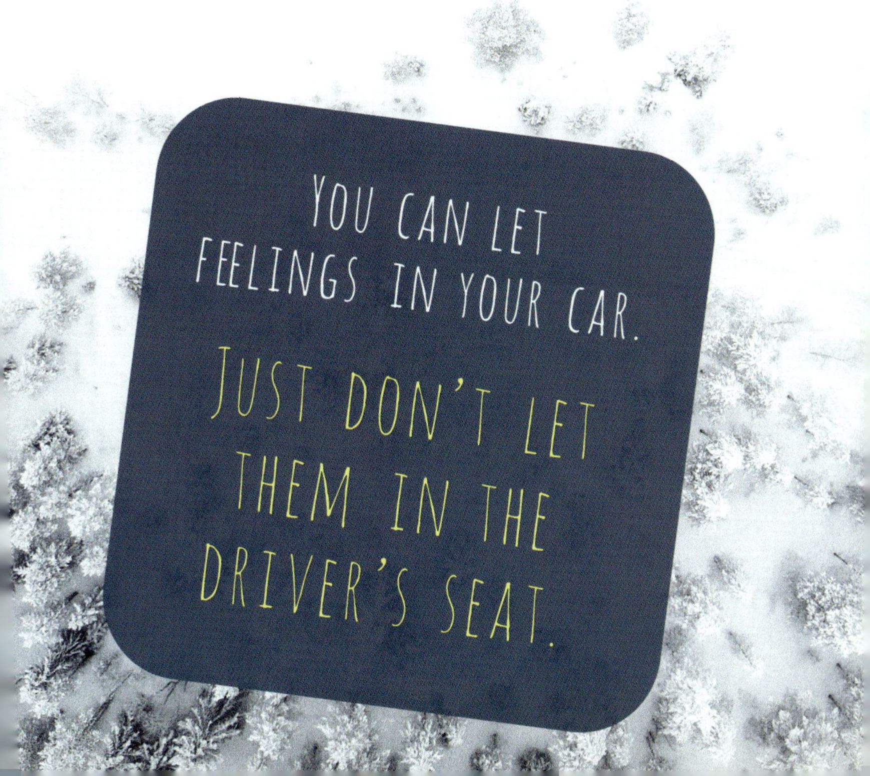

YOU CAN LET
FEELINGS IN YOUR CAR.
JUST DON'T LET
THEM IN THE
DRIVER'S SEAT.

DECEMBER

8

A fool vents all his feelings,
but a wise man holds them back.
Proverbs 29:11

IT'S HARD
TO SEE CLEARLY
THROUGH THE
DISTORTION
OF EMOTION

DECEMBER

9

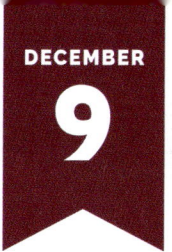

A fool vents all his feelings,
but a wise man holds them back.

Proverbs 29:11

CHOICES LEAD. FEELINGS FOLLOW.

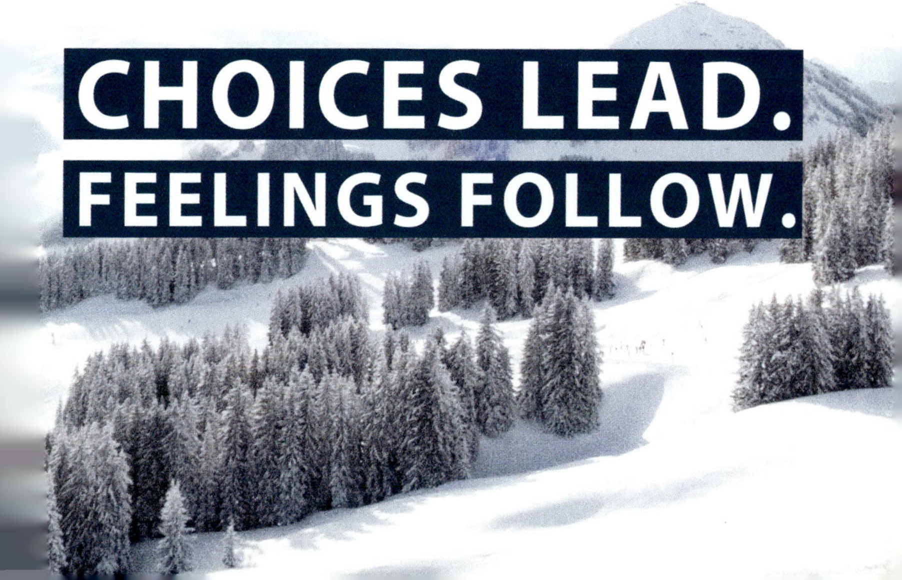

DECEMBER
10

If a ruler pays attention to lies,
all his servants become wicked.
Proverbs 29:12

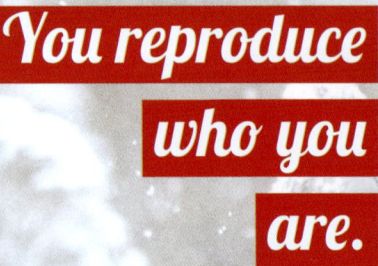

You don't reproduce what you want. You reproduce who you are.

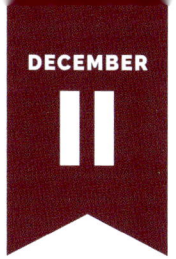

The rod and rebuke give wisdom,
but a child left to himself
brings shame to his mother.

Proverbs 29:15

**THE GOAL OF CHILD-TRAINING
IS NOT JUST FOR
MISBEHAVIOR TO STOP,
BUT FOR THE
RIGHT BEHAVIOR TO BEGIN.**

DECEMBER

12

Correct your son, and he will give you rest.
Yes, he will give delight to your soul.
Proverbs 29:17

CORRECTION
IS NOT REJECTION
BUT PROTECTION
AND DIRECTION

Correct your son, and he will give you rest.
Yes, he will give delight to your soul.
Proverbs 29:17

**GOOD PARENTING
DOES NOT HAPPEN
ACCIDENTALLY.
GOOD PARENTING
HAPPENS
INTENTIONALLY.**

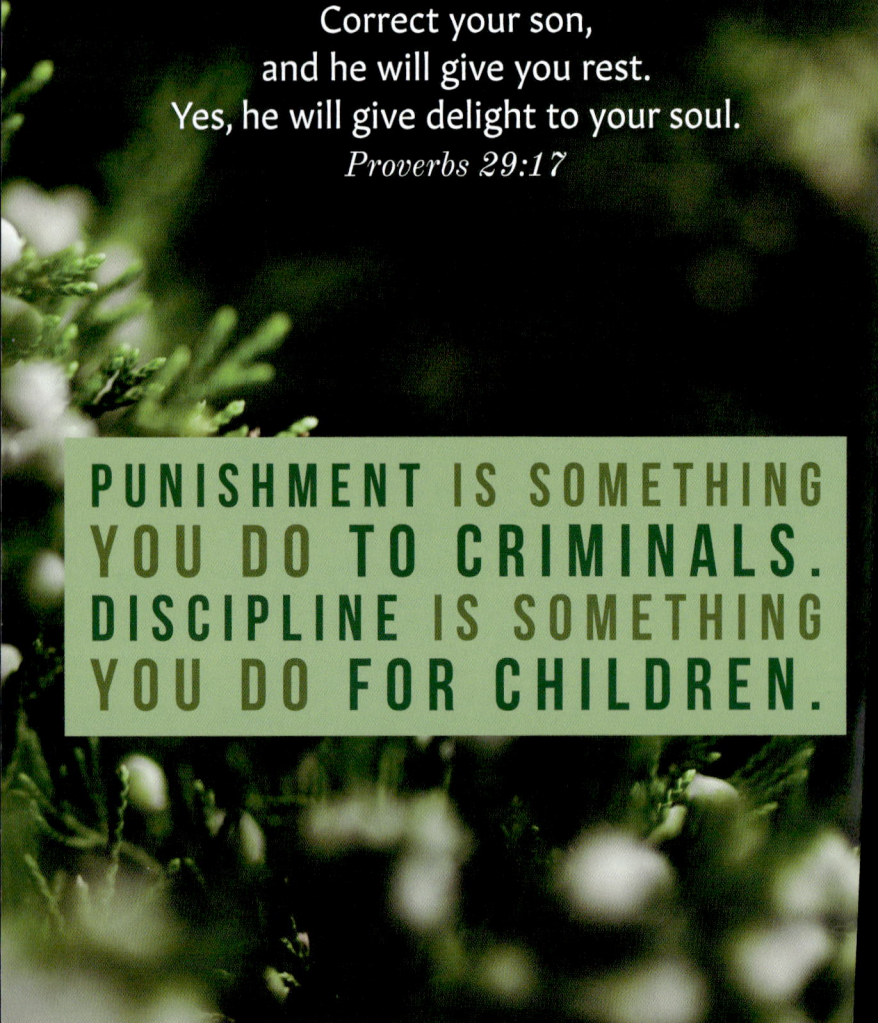

Correct your son,
and he will give you rest.
Yes, he will give delight to your soul.

Proverbs 29:17

PUNISHMENT IS SOMETHING
YOU DO TO CRIMINALS.
DISCIPLINE IS SOMETHING
YOU DO FOR CHILDREN.

DECEMBER

15

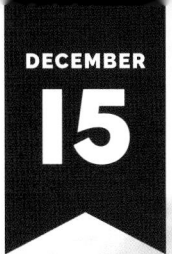

Where there is no revelation,
the people cast off restraint,
but happy is he who keeps the law.

Proverbs 29:18

NEVER LET VISION FRUSTRATE YOU

ALWAYS LET VISION MOTIVATE YOU

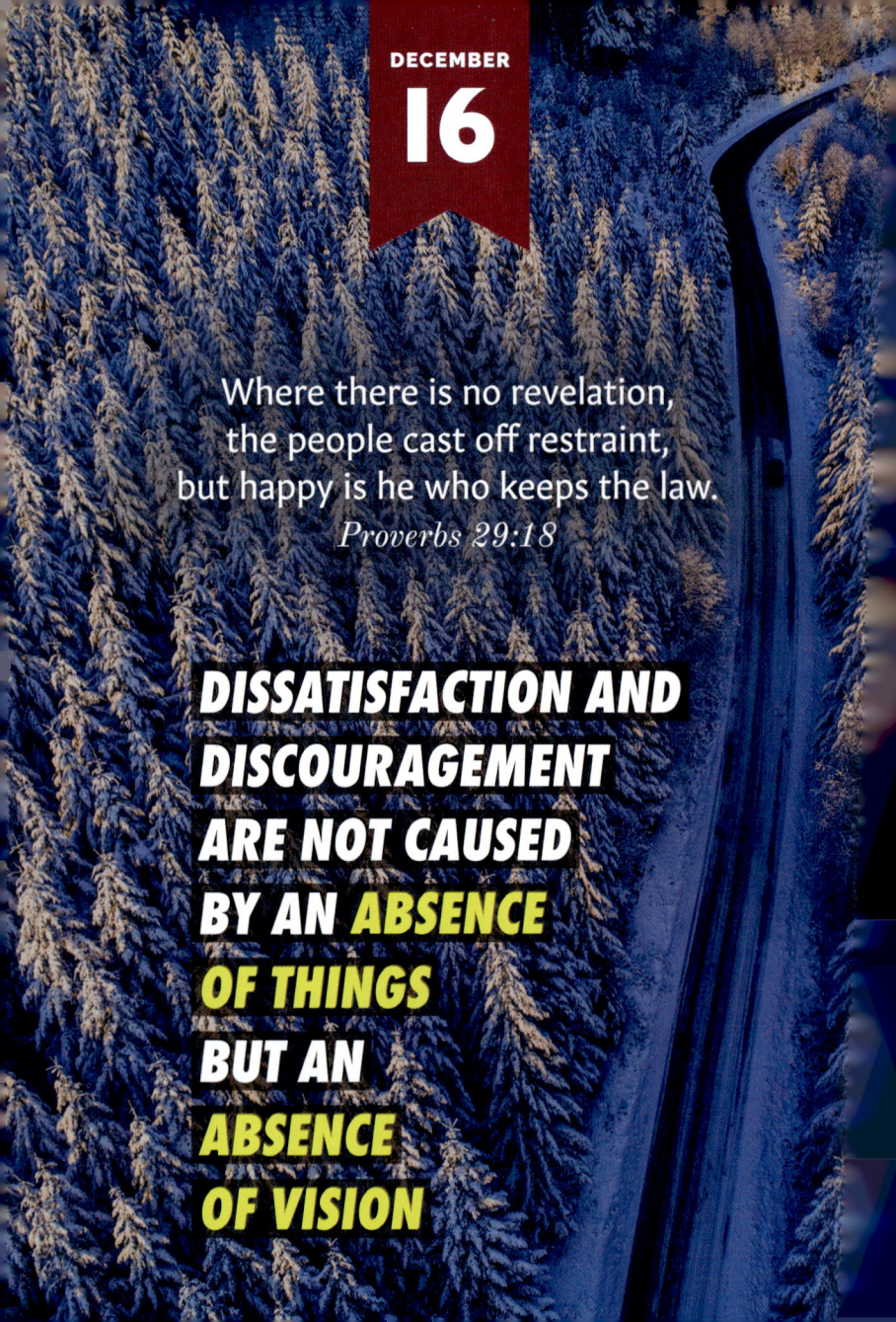

DECEMBER
16

Where there is no revelation,
the people cast off restraint,
but happy is he who keeps the law.
Proverbs 29:18

DISSATISFACTION AND DISCOURAGEMENT ARE NOT CAUSED BY AN ABSENCE OF THINGS BUT AN ABSENCE OF VISION

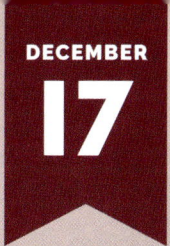

DECEMBER
17

Where there is no revelation,
the people cast off restraint,
but happy is he who keeps the law.
Proverbs 29:18

VISUALIZE
TOMORROW
—
VALUE
TODAY

DECEMBER

18

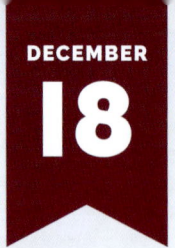

Where there is no revelation,
the people cast off restraint,
but happy is he who keeps the law.

Proverbs 29:18

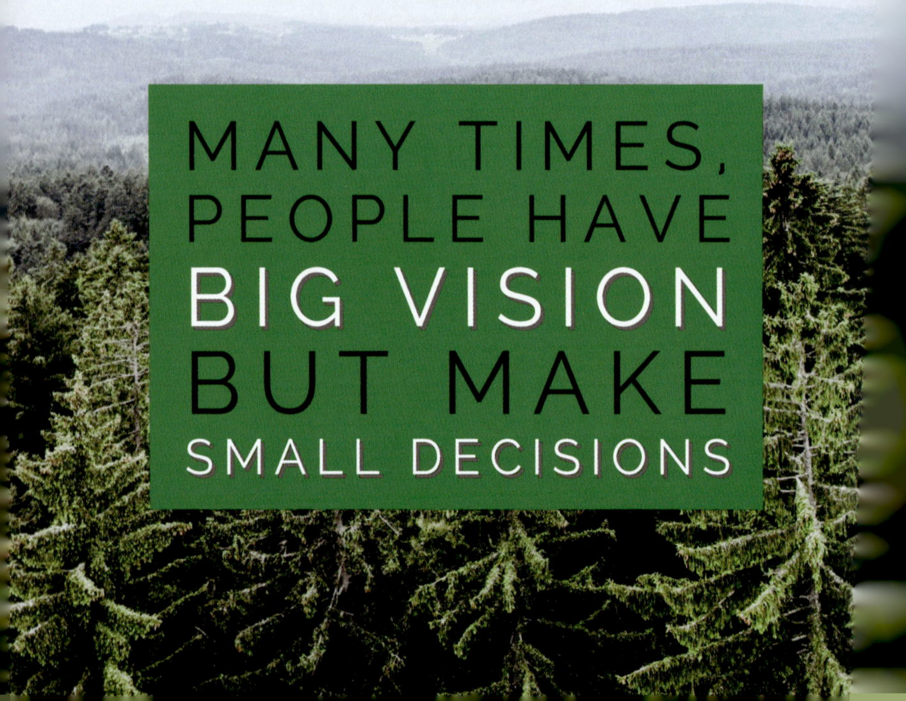

MANY TIMES, PEOPLE HAVE BIG VISION BUT MAKE SMALL DECISIONS

DECEMBER

19

Where there is no revelation,
the people cast off restraint,
but happy is he who keeps the law.
Proverbs 29:18

YOU HAVE TO MAKE
DECISIONS THAT
MATCH THE
SIZE OF YOUR
VISION

DECEMBER
20

Where there is no revelation,
the people cast off restraint,
but happy is he who keeps the law.
Proverbs 29:18

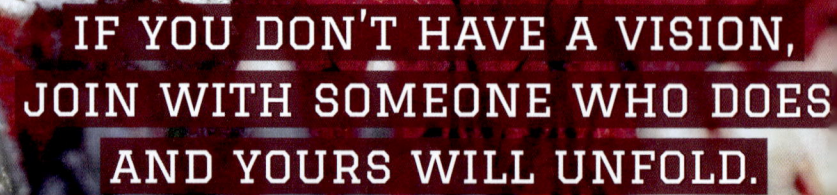

IF YOU DON'T HAVE A VISION,
JOIN WITH SOMEONE WHO DOES
AND YOURS WILL UNFOLD.

DECEMBER
21

Do you see a man hasty in his words?
There is more hope for a fool
than for him.

Proverbs 29:20

YOU GET INTO TROUBLE
WHEN YOU SAY
OUT OF YOUR TROUBLE

Do you see a man hasty in his words?
There is more hope for a fool than for him.
Proverbs 29:20

In a crisis,
the first thing
out of your mouth
will set either
your miracle
or your mess
into motion.

The fear of man brings a snare,
but whoever trusts in the LORD shall be safe.

Proverbs 29:25

*You'll never find peace
in another man's head*

The fear of man brings a snare,
but whoever trusts in the LORD shall be safe.

Proverbs 29:25

NEVER WORSHIP AT THE ALTAR OF ANOTHER MAN'S OPINION

The fear of man brings a snare,
but whoever trusts in the LORD shall be safe.

Proverbs 29:25

DON'T LIVE YOUR LIFE

BASED ON WHAT OTHERS THINK OF YOU.

LIVE YOUR LIFE

THINKING OF OTHERS.

The fear of man brings a snare,
but whoever trusts in the LORD shall be safe.

Proverbs 29:25

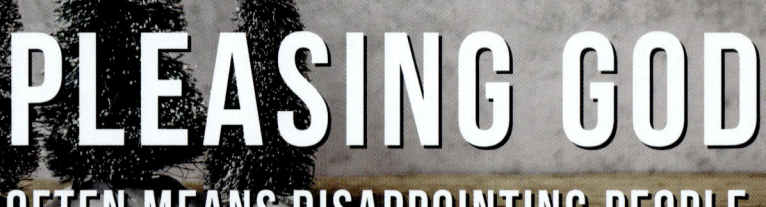

PLEASING GOD

OFTEN MEANS DISAPPOINTING PEOPLE.

DECEMBER

27

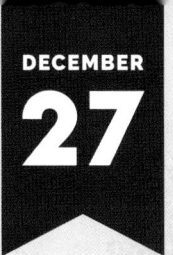

The fear of man brings a snare,
but whoever trusts in the LORD shall be safe.

Proverbs 29:25

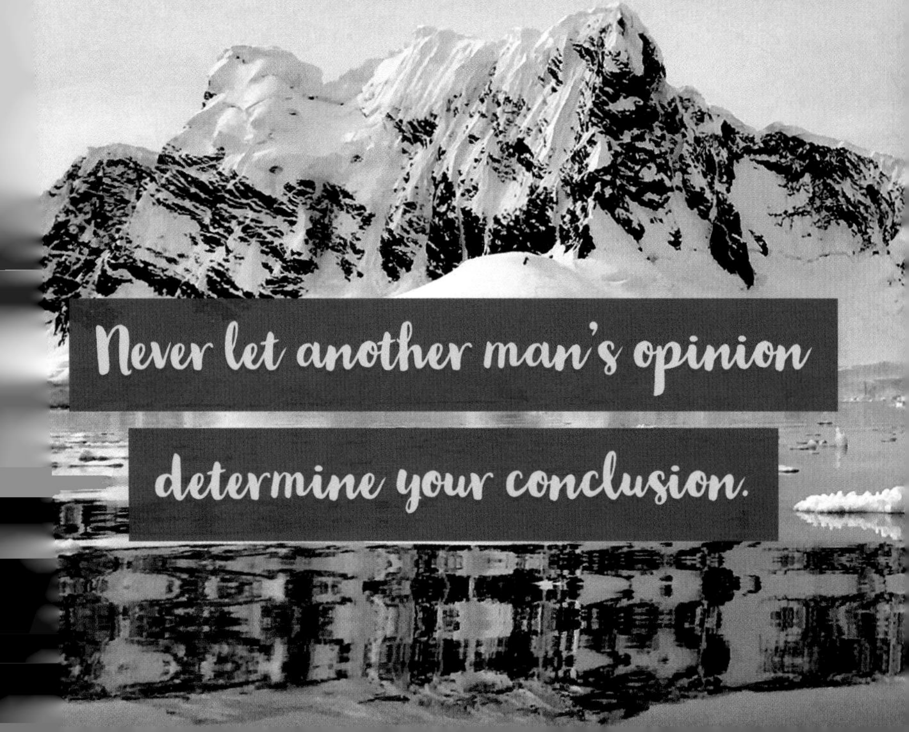
Never let another man's opinion
determine your conclusion.

Many seek the ruler's favor,
but justice for man
comes from the LORD.

Proverbs 29:26

WHEN YOU'RE ACCEPTED
BY THE BEST,
WHO CARES ABOUT THE REST?

DECEMBER

29

Every word of God is pure.
He is a shield to those
who put their trust in Him.
Proverbs 30:5

EXPECT A BRIGHT FUTURE
TOMORROW
BY BELIEVING GOD'S WORD
TODAY

DECEMBER
30

Every word of God is pure.
He is a shield to those who put their trust in Him.
Do not add to His words lest He rebuke you,
and you be found a liar.

Proverbs 30:5-6

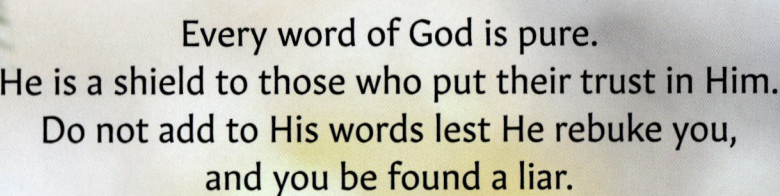

IF YOU BELIEVE WHAT YOU LIKE IN THE BIBLE
BUT DON'T BELIEVE WHAT YOU DON'T LIKE,
IT'S NOT THE BIBLE YOU TRUST IN.
IT'S YOURSELF.

DECEMBER
31

Do not add to His words lest He rebuke you,
and you be found a liar.

Proverbs 30:6

DON'T PLAY IN GRAY AREAS
WHEN YOU HAVE A
BLACK-AND-WHITE BIBLE

GOD LOVES YOU

AS IF YOU WERE

THE ONLY

PERSON

IN THIS WORLD

TO LOVE!

HOW TO START THE MOST IMPORTANT RELATIONSHIP OF YOUR LIFE

Shark fishing is my hobby. I use a kayak to paddle my bait hundreds of yards into the ocean, then paddle back and fish from the shore. Some time ago, I was in the middle of a four-hour battle with a very large shark, and a crowd had gathered from around the beach to see what I was going to reel in! A man in the crowd struck up a conversation with me while I was battling this shark. He asked me what I did for a living, and I told him I was a pastor.

When people discover that I am pastor, I get a variety of responses. This man's response was unusual. He simply blurted out with disdain, "Well, I hate organized religion!" I replied, "Me too." He was surprised at my reply, so I continued, asking, "Do you know who else hates organized religion?" Before he could respond, I shocked him further and said, "Jesus!" Now, I had this fellow's undivided attention, and I hope that I now have yours as well.

You see, Christianity is not about religion. It is about a relationship with a loving, heavenly Father through His one Son, Jesus Christ.

I believe that you have a figurative homing beacon on the inside of you, placed there by the God who created you. It is a spiritual hole, if you will, that can only be filled by God.

I understand this personally. Before I entered into a relationship with Jesus, I tried to fill that hole with women, alcohol, and fighting. It was fun for a while, but when the fun was over, and the things I tried to fill that vacuum with came crashing down around me, I still had that homing beacon on the inside of me. It was my heavenly Father, gently, patiently, and ever so lovingly calling me home.

Maybe you can sense the emptiness on the inside of you and the loving call of your heavenly Father, imploring you to come home. Why not surrender your life to Him and find the joy, peace, and purpose you've been looking for all your life? Why not start the most important relationship of your life? It's so simple, but life transforming.

Please pray this prayer with me. Repeat it out loud, but mean it from your heart. I discovered a long time ago that when you reach out to God from your heart, He will always reach back to you with His love.

Pray this simple prayer with me now:

> "Father God, I come to you now. Sin, I turn my back on you. Jesus, I turn to You now. I believe you were raised from the dead just for me. Come into my heart, and be my LORD. I surrender my life to you today. I enter into a relationship with you today!"

If you prayed that prayer, please contact us here at Joy Church, and let us know that you started the most important relationship of your life. We want to respect your privacy and dignity, but we also want to give you some information to help you walk out this new relationship in a life-giving way!

You can email us at mail@joychurchinternational.org or give us a call at 615-773-5252. You can write to us at Joy Church, P.O. Box 247, Mount Juliet, TN, 37121.

If you live in or are visiting the Nashville/Mount Juliet, TN area, we would love to invite you to join us for one of our upcoming services. For more information and directions, please visit our website at www.joychurch.net. We look forward to hearing from you!

Please remember that God loves you as if you were the only person in this world to love!

Jim Frease and his wife, Anne, and their son, Johnathan.

ABOUT THE AUTHOR

Jim Frease is the founder and senior pastor of Joy Church in Mt. Juliet, Tennessee, and founder and president of World Changers Bible Institute.

He is also the founder of Joy Ministerial Exchange, a ministerial organization designed to impart to pastors from across the country.

Jim emphasizes a relationship with Jesus Christ, not religion; the Word of God, not tradition; and enjoying life, not enduring it. He teaches not just what to do, but how.

Jim and his wife, Anne, have been married since 1990, and they deeply love their son, Johnathan. Jim loves spending time with his family, and he enjoys Ohio State football and fishing. Anne loves to shop. Sometimes, they compromise and shop at Bass Pro Shops®.

Most importantly, Jim and Anne are deeply in love with the Lord Jesus Christ and are completely committed to His Word. As they minister, they do so with humor & joy (Nehemiah 8:10) and integrity (Psalm 26:11), propelling the listener to a greater intimacy with Jesus.

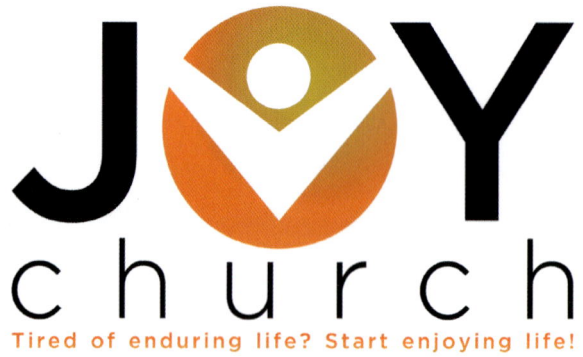

Tired of enduring life? Start enjoying life!

ABOUT JOY CHURCH

Based out of Mt. Juliet, Tennessee,
Joy Church is a rapidly growing, multigenerational,
multicultural church with people from almost every
denominational background—including those with
no church background at all.

At Joy Church, we don't believe in organized religion.
We believe in an organized relationship with
God the Father through His Son, Jesus Christ.

We are not about tradition
but the liberating Word of God.

We are not about enduring life.
We are about enjoying life!

For more information, please visit joychurch.net

KNOWLEDGE IS THE ACCUMULATION OF INFORMATION.

WISDOM IS THE CORRECT APPLICATION OF THAT INFORMATION.

No matter where you are in life, I think we can all agree that we could always use more wisdom.

The Bible tells us in Proverbs 4:7, "Wisdom is the principal thing, therefore get wisdom." You are the sum total of the decisions you make, who you are today is a direct result of your choices yesterday, and the decisions you are making today directly affect your tomorrow.

This book is designed to enhance your decision making, raise your standard of living, and give you wisdom 365 days of the year!

Jim Frease is the founder and senior pastor of Joy Church as well as founder and president of World Changers Bible Institute in Mt. Juliet, TN. Jim has been in the ministry since 1984 and is known as a pastor to pastors, a trainer of leaders, and has ministered around the country and internationally. Most importantly, he is deeply in love with the Lord Jesus Christ and is completely committed to His Word! Pastor Jim lives in the Nashville area with his wife and best friend Anne, and their son Johnathan.

www.joychurch.net

SBN 978-0-9983918-8-5   US$15.00
51500
9 780998 391885